RELOCATION IN URBAN PLANNING:
FROM OBSTACLE TO OPPORTUNITY

ENVIRONMENTAL STUDIES SERIES
OF THE UNIVERSITY OF PENNSYLVANIA

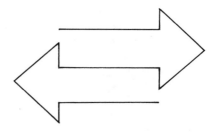

Relocation in urban planning: from obstacle to opportunity

PAUL L. NIEBANCK

WITH THE ASSISTANCE OF MARK R. YESSIAN

Final report of the study of the relocation of elderly persons
Chester Rapkin, director

University of Pennsylvania Press
Philadelphia 1968

Copyright © 1968
by the Trustees
of the University of Pennsylvania

Library of Congress Catalog Card
Number 68-21556
7566

Manufactured in the
United States of America

GENERAL INTRODUCTION

To commit oneself to the exploration of man's environment is to undertake an important intellectual task. To commit oneself to the improvement of that environment is to accept a high responsibility. The concerns of one often have relevance to the other, and there can be fruitful collaboration between them.

The Environmental Studies Series will enlist the energies of both the concerned academician and the dedicated professional to gain new insights into the natural and man-made environment. Scholarly works will be included in the Series, but the subjects to which they are addressed must be timely and of a high social priority. The wisdom of professional activists will contribute to the Series, but not at the sacrifice of scholarly comprehensiveness and rigor.

The unifying theme of the Series is explicit in the general title— Environmental Studies. No major aspect of our urbanized society will be overlooked, and no opportunity for the reporting of cross-disciplinary research will be ignored. It is hoped that, as the Series progresses, a contribution will be made to correcting the current difficulty among scholars of applying knowledge from various fields to urgent environmental problems.

Man's environment is rich and it has been greatly studied. In sponsoring the Series, the Institute plans to present the most logically reasoned, the most useful, and the most relevant of the manuscripts that it explores and develops. The current volume initiating the Series, we believe, is successful in meeting these criteria. Drawing on extensive research, *Relocation in Urban Planning* deals with a problem that man has brought upon himself and proposes a positive set of alternative policies. Other studies in the Series will deal with equally timely issues, such as the police and community conflict, the subject of the next volume now under preparation.

Philadelphia
March 27, 1968

Institute for Environmental Studies
G. Holmes Perkins
Chairman, Research Council

CONTENTS

PREFACE

It will be a long time before this country is likely to try once again to clear large sections of our older residential districts in an effort to cope with the problems that beset its cities and their citizens.

A statement as sweeping as this could not have been made even a few years ago when redevelopment policy was still quite insensitive to the basic causes of slums and the needs of the persons who inhabit them. Now, however, the kinds of redevelopment programs that disregard the values of the people they displace are encountering strong resistance, and the urban renewal program, for one, is much more inclined than in the past to give primacy to the desires and needs of these persons.

By the mid-1960's, fully a quarter of a million residents each year were being forced by public authorities to make way for highways, other public improvements and private undertakings of all kinds. Substantial numbers of these dislodged persons were elderly. The elderly have been found to be somewhat more vulnerable to the shocks and losses attendant on relocation, and to suffer more intensely from the pressure of poverty in its various forms than their younger counterparts. It was to this elderly sector of the relocation population that the attention of the Ford Foundation was directed in 1962, and the Foundation's concern found expression through the study of which this volume is a product. The study itself paralleled the work of several other research efforts and was conducted at a time when relocation practice was undergoing a substantial amount of internal change. The coincidence of administrative reform with citizen awakening thus placed this study in a context of hope rather than one of despair.

The study consisted primarily of four demonstration projects, conducted in San Antonio, San Francisco, Providence, and New York, each of which has been described in detail in an earlier publication. Two additional volumes have reported on the background research. The present volume constitutes the final report of the project and, although it draws on a considerable amount of new material, it reflects the theme and findings of all the previous work.

The preparation of this volume was dependent, directly or indirectly, on the work of many persons. Not the least of these were the directors of the demonstration projects and their respective staffs and volunteers. To work with such people as these was a great privilege. Their work was beset with many difficulties and frustrations. Their reward is the knowledge that the lives of countless additional persons will be rendered less difficult because of the continued influence of their efforts on social policy.

What merit this study may possess is also the result of the perseverance and imagination of the research staff at the Institute for Environmental Studies. Again, it has been particularly rewarding to work with a group with such able minds and strong commitment. Special thanks go to Paul L. Niebanck and Grace Milgram, Assistant Directors of the study, and to Mary K. Nenno, Director of Field Operations, who gave unstintingly of their time and talent over the entire course of the long project.

The study is concluded in trust that its findings will prove helpful to policymakers and program administrators at many levels, and with the hope that it will add in some measure to the body of knowledge in the field of urban studies.

Chester Rapkin
Professor of City Planning
University of Pennsylvania

1

INTRODUCTION

Only two generations ago, ours was still very much a rural nation, and even in the densely settled areas, systems of values and modes of behavior were greatly colored by our rural past. The Depression of the 1930's and the two decades that followed World War II have changed these conditions and have begun to change the images as well. The process of urbanization is virtually complete. Rapid change is no longer a startling phenomenon. Adaptation to change and anticipation of change have become principles of public policy. Ameliorating the negative effects of rapid change and capitalizing on the opportunities that it presents are vital concerns of the day.

The very notion of urban redevelopment is comparatively new to our vocabulary. A few decades ago, the felt need for large public investments in our urban centers was comparatively slight and was shared by only a tiny minority of the population. Furthermore, it was assumed that most of the hardships that were experienced by urban dwellers were matters of temporary necessity and largely the responsibility of the affected person or his family to resolve. Especially since the late 1940's, these attitudes have undergone a radical transformation, and the expression of a newer, more realistic and relevant set of values is everywhere to be seen. Transportation and communications systems have matured. Huge public investments have begun to make the city a more efficient and productive place to live and work. And, while there has been a decided time lag between the initiation of changes in the physical environment and the initiation of changes in the political, economic, and social systems themselves, the latter have begun to respond as well.

Involuntary relocation has been a by-product of the massive physical changes that have now become an integral part of our progressive society. In order to accomplish what had been necessary and overcome what had been neglected so long, large numbers of persons have been forced to move from their homes, often at great cost, and usually with altogether too little assistance by the institutions that caused them to be dislodged. The poorest and weakest members of society thereby have paid the highest cost for improvements undertaken by governmental agencies for the general welfare, in whose benefit they usually have not shared directly at all.

This, however, is not the full story. Through the efforts of responsible lawmakers and administrators, representative pressure groups, and *ad hoc* organizations of the people themselves, substantial improvements have been instituted in relocation policy. Many thoughtful persons now recognize that relocation—or rehousing, which is not only a more palatable but also coming to be a more proper description—contains possibilities for real human service and has unique qualities that permit it to rectify in one motion many of the inequities that presently exist and remedy many of the ills that seem to persist.

The present volume is a product of the concerns that a decade ago were labeled "the human side of urban renewal," and that today are being reflected in social unrest and militant demands for immediate readjustment in the list of national priorities. Thus, while the study, in its particulars, is concerned with the elderly population and with relocation caused by the urban renewal program, it cannot be viewed in proper perspective without some consideration of much larger issues. It is the entire set of redevelopment programs, taken as a whole, that has been the primary public vehicle for adapting the city to the changing demands put upon it, and these same programs have been the cause of hardship and the symbol of societal neglect for not merely the elderly, but for many other persons and institutions as well.

THE STRUCTURE OF THE BOOK

The material is presented in five sections. Chapter Two surveys the advances that have been made in relocation policy, particularly at the national level, since large-scale redevelopment became a factor on the urban scene. This material draws from a variety of sources, but relies heavily on changes in the law and administrative rulings and directives.

The third chapter describes the elderly population that is subject to displacement and evaluates its ability to deal with the rigors of urban life. Drawing on the earlier work of this research project, it catalogs the major classes of programs now in existence that either do or could serve the needs of the relocatee and others like him.

Chapter Four reviews the four demonstration projects that were associated with this study, each of which is reported at length in an earlier volume. The projects are described in turn, and the most important common findings are then put forward.

Chapter Five is intended as a comprehensive statement of recommendations, some of a general and long-range nature and others of specific and immediate concern. The idea that relocation is more properly viewed as an opportunity than as a necessary evil is explored here, and the limitations on that thought are examined.

The volume closes with a brief statement of the important gaps in knowledge that still remain to be filled. While it might be argued that successful relocation is more dependent on the commitment of the worker and the allocation of public funds than on research findings, there are at least a few important matters about which we should know much more.

A WORD OF CAUTION

In the research endeavor leading to this volume, it was difficult to separate specific findings from broad understandings. Indeed, had the research findings been entirely limited to the concerns that gave the study birth, a number of more fundamental matters would have been bypassed altogether. In one sense, the principal findings of the study go far beyond the questions that were posed at the outset. Whereas a set of palliative measures could have been produced to deal moderately well with individual cases as they arise, any real solutions to the problems whose symptoms are exposed in the course of relocation can only take the form of significant changes in the institutional behavior patterns that cause the lesser problems to arise at all. Despite signs of real reform, most of these patterns have persisted, and have resulted in public programs that inevitably lead to the direct satisfaction of the desires of the more privileged groups and to the neglect of the less privileged.

Thus it is that the most responsible program that could be suggested by the research team that undertook this study would be one that set out purposefully and systematically to serve the housing and related needs of the deprived sectors of the urban population generally. Specific improvements in relocation practice, although hardly without merit, were seen as of lesser long-run importance. This general finding is set forth at the outset so as to provide the sympathetic reader with a context in which to view the particulars in the text, and to lay bare before the critical reader the point of view that developed in the course of the research. That attitude can be summarized as follows:

1. The redevelopment of our cities, whether clothed in incidental efforts to assist the persons it has displaced or openly contemptuous of their interests, has involved great costs to them. These costs, moreover, have not been entirely confined to the "losses" that are ordinarily associated with relocation. They must also be measured in terms of the regressive effects of redevelopment policy and the obstructionist responses on the part of the people whom redevelopment has chosen *not* to serve. Whether particular individuals are directly harmed is not at issue, but perhaps more important is the dramatic evidence that the groups that redevelopment has chosen as its beneficiaries are usually not those in the greatest need of the benefits that redevelopment can offer.

2. Some would argue that a discontinuance of redevelopment is the proper answer. It is held here that such a policy is neither necessary nor desirable. The issue is not so neatly drawn; it is not a matter of the redevelopment tool itself, but rather of how and on whose behalf the tool is wielded.

3. The relevant long-run answer is a substantial shift in policy, one that would give great weight to the needs of people who are currently carrying the burden of redevelopment. Redevelopment would become a vehicle for an equalization in the distribution of valued objects as well as a means to the enhancement of the general welfare.

4. Were this shift not to come about, or were it delayed, there are nevertheless a large number of important reforms that could

be instituted and that in the aggregate could considerably reduce the net human costs of redevelopment. Even if the basic redevelopment policies were changed in the manner suggested in (3), above, these refinements would still be needed. Hence, as might realistically be expected, these matters are reported fully in the text. Nevertheless, the underlying theme is repeatedly made explicit, and it is always implicit, and the reader is forewarned.

2

CHAPTER

THE GROWING CONCERN FOR
ADEQUATE RELOCATION

Within a rather short time, relocation has become a major concern to persons involved in physical development and social welfare planning. As an adjunct to physical change, it often inhibits the pace and effectiveness of redevelopment. As a welfare tool, it often brings to the surface problems that were invisible prior to the intervention. As an imposition on the household, it often causes or precipitates problems, some of which are insoluble. As a program affecting older areas, it often places particular hardships on precisely those sectors of the population who are least able to deal with them and who are most in need of help: the elderly, the small businessmen, the indigent, the minority groups. Finally, as a program without a life of its own, relocation is difficult to deal with either in a conceptual or a practical sense. Nevertheless, through an intricate and slow process of trial and error and reaction to political pressure, significant changes have occurred in relocation since its inception as a systematic public program.

SMALL BEGINNINGS

Before the Great Depression of the 1930's, large-scale urban redevelopment was hardly more than a subject for drawing room conversation. Conditions were ripe at neither the federal nor the local level for major public investments in urban improvement. The Depression changed these conditions, and for the first time, such programs as slum clearance and public housing received national attention.

Although large for the times, the anti-Depression measures were modest by today's standards. The number of people who were dislodged by redevelopment was relatively small, and the incidence of hardship was scattered and unnoticed. Federal laws governing the programs that involved displacement demanded no special assistance to the affected households, and with the wide-spread availability of vacant units neither state nor local jurisdictions felt it necessary to fill the breach. Where help was offered, it was usually by local welfare agencies, which provided guidance and occasional financial aid. Otherwise, it was assumed, often correctly, that satisfactory rehousing could easily be found, and that the move itself was not a burden.[1]

The first federal legislation to specify a concern for the displaced household, albeit an indirect one, was the Housing Act of 1937, which established the United States Housing Authority. The Act established the principle of "equivalent elimination," but allowed local authorities to waive the principle in instances where low-cost housing was in short supply:

> . . . no capital grant shall be made for the development of any low-rent housing or slum clearance project involving the construction of new dwellings unless the project includes the elimination by demolition, condemnation, and effective closing, or the compulsory repair or improvement of unsafe or unsanitary dwellings . . . substantially equal in number to the number of newly constructed dwelling units provided by the project; except that such elimination may, in the discretion of the Authority, be deferred . . . where the shortage of decent, safe, or sanitary housing available to families is so acute as to force dangerous overcrowding of such families.[2]

A careful reading of this section reveals that the demolition of slum units rather than the relocation of families was the primary concern of the time. Instead of stressing that a replacement must be constructed for each unit demolished, the emphasis was the reverse: that there must be a unit demolished for each new one

---

1. For a more thorough review of the early days of urban development, see Martin Millspaugh, "Problems and Opportunities of Relocation," *Law and Contemporary Problems,* XXVI (Winter, 1961), pp. 6-36; and Jewel Bellush and Murray Hausknecht, "Urban Renewal: An Historical Overview," in *Urban Renewal: People, Politics and Planning,* Jewel Bellush and Murray Hausknecht, Eds. (Garden City, New York: Doubleday, 1967), pp. 3-16.

2. U.S., *Statutes at Large,* L, Part 1, 891-892.

built. Furthermore, there was no mention of the cost, quality, or location of the relocation housing, although the sponsor of the Act, Sen. Robert F. Wagner, had made some attempt to provide such standards.[3]

Despite its obvious weaknesses, the new legislation marked a significant first step. Slum housing was to be replaced with new housing for slum occupants, and clearance might even be deferred if adequate rehousing was not available. Moreover, through an administrative directive of the Housing Authority, all local housing agencies were urged in general terms to consider providing some assistance in relocating the families that were displaced by public housing projects. As time went on, the federal agency set forth procedures by which local action might be guided.[4] Recognition was given to such factors as the need for citizen advisory committees, social agency cooperation, good record-keeping, and follow-up services. The procedures listed in the manuals of the late 1930's sound familiar today, and while they were stated in comparatively harsh and insensitive terms, they were essentially the basis for subsequent operations.

PRELUDE TO 1949

During the years of World War II, relocation activity was reduced to a near standstill. What residential construction there was, was built on vacant land, and clearance was infrequent. But the construction boom that followed the war again involved large amounts of displacement, and, where this displacement was part and parcel of publicly sponsored redevelopment, relocation once again became a public concern. Conferences were held on relocation policies. Reports on relocation experience proliferated. Gradually, the size and nature of the task came to be recognized, and methods to cope with it tested.

Signs of this increased sophistication and responsibility were readily apparent. Many local authorities, often for the first time, began to maintain current information on housing vacancies. The

3. See Citizens Housing Council of New York, *Report and Recommendations of the Committee on Rehousing of Tenants,* 1938.
4. See United States Housing Authority, *Relocation of Site Occupants in Slum Clearance Projects,* 1939.

caliber of relocation personnel was seen to be important, and the term "professional relocation worker" was even tossed about. Although relocation was still seen basically as a means of expediting the redevelopment process, a real interest in the needs and wishes of the relocatees themselves was often evinced. Finally, there was a budding recognition that, in order to achieve humane and effective redevelopment, full cooperative planning among relocation, housing, and social service agencies was a necessity.

Most of these developments, to be sure, relate to thoughts rather than actions, but the insights gained in the immediate postwar years did manifest themselves in some program innovations. Site offices were sometimes established; occupancy surveys were increasingly broadened to include sociological data and personal attitudes; the aid of neighborhood committees was occasionally enlisted; tenant education was more conspicuous; and a philosophy of outreach slowly began to supplant the tendency to wait for the tenant to express his own needs. As the relocation effort became more complex and service-oriented, it also achieved a certain amount of independent status in many communities, and in so doing it was able to command some of the cooperation and assistance from the housing and social welfare officials that it so desperately needed.

The experience of the Stuyvesant Town project in New York was exemplary of the postwar advances in relocation philosophy and technique. Although its racially discriminatory rental policies besmirched its reputation, in respect to relocation this large project, carried out immediately after the war by the Metropolitan Life Insurance Co., has become a milestone in the annals of city building. It involved a rapid awakening to the necessity for intensive assistance, and typified the relocation problem as it was then coming to be known. "Here was the fabled melting pot in real life. . . . Here also were families rooted in the area for generations. . . ."[5] The report of the relocation staff, reflecting a kind of sensitivity that had rarely been witnessed in other programs, concluded that:

> By forcing people from one slum to another, the basic ills of most urban low-rent housing will merely be shifted to a different

5. Tenant Relocation Bureau, Inc., *Three Thousand Families Move to Make Way for Stuyvesant Town* (New York, 1946), p. 2.

location. If urban redevelopment is going to benefit the entire city, the needs of families living on slum sites must be given consideration through long-range planning. Whatever the overall plan, a human approach to the tenants' needs is the true function of a Tenant Relocation Bureau.[6]

An important by-product of the relocation efforts of the 1940's is the fact that the plight of the urban poor became exposed. The precondemnation site survey became a vehicle, although usually one unintended for general use, for obtaining a better knowledge of the severe problems facing many residents of our cities. One site survey even went so far as to delve into the fatalism and apparent good humor that were typical of the residents to be displaced.[7] Few meaningful recommendations were drawn from these surveys, but they still served as a source of minimal understanding that had been almost wholly lacking before then.

THE HOUSING ACT OF 1949

In 1949, the federal government made its first major response to the condition of American cities since the public housing program had been initiated in 1937. The principal tool for rebuilding the city came to be known simply as "Title I," and it presaged an amount of clearance and human displacement far greater than had been the case under the public housing program or any combination of programs in the past.

While the stated goals of the Housing Act of 1949 centered on the provision of a decent home in a suitable living environment for every American family, Title I itself was more typically used to clear slums and excite private initiative in the reconstruction effort. Thus the clearance programs in most cities reflected the various desires of the established interests more than they did the housing needs of the poor. There being no companion housing program of sufficient size to absorb the displaced households, the clearance programs themselves bore the responsibility, in the minds of the critics, for America's failure to achieve its stated housing objectives. It is in this context that the development of relocation since 1949 must be viewed.

The Congressional hearings preliminary to the passage of the

---

6. *Ibid.,* p. 22.
7. See St. Louis Housing Authority, *Tenant Relocation,* 2 vols., 1941.

1949 Act dealt with a wide range of issues relating to relocation.[8] Some of the points of discussion were quite basic, and one in particular stands out as having a marked effect on the progress of relocation since the Act was passed. It revolved around the proper role of the federal government in the provision or production of housing for displaced families and other households of limited means. Such people as John B. Blandford, Jr., Philip M. Klutznick, and Raymond M. Foley made the case for a strong federal role in these matters, and indeed expressed the belief that the success of the entire redevelopment program would rest in large part on the availability or production of housing for the displaced families.[9]

The spirit that won the day, however, was that the local government should take the responsibility for assuring decent housing for families evicted because of redevelopment. The federal stake in adequate relocation housing, under the Title I program, was thus restricted to requiring that localities provide the needed replacement units. No positive program—not even public housing—was initiated or expanded to the degree necessary to make sure that such units became available. The pleas of Blandford, Klutznick, and Foley were acknowledged in that the Act specifically called for adequate and equivalent replacement housing within the financial means of the relocatees. There were even provisions that a new neighborhood be reasonably near the displaced person's place of work and be desirable in terms of its utilities and facilities. Yet the onus for these vast responsibilities was placed almost entirely on the limited resources of the localities:

> Contracts for financial aid shall be made only with a duly authorized local public agency and shall require that—
> . . . (c) There be a feasible method for the temporary relocation of families displaced from the project area, and that there are or are being provided, in the project area or in other areas not generally less desirable in regard to public utilities and public and com-

---

8. See, for example, U.S. Congress, Senate, Special Committee on Post-War Economic Policy and Planning, *Hearings, on Housing and Urban Redevelopment*, 79th Cong., 1st Sess., 1945; and U.S. Congress, House, Committee on Banking and Currency, *Hearings, on H.R. 4009*, 81st Cong., 1st Sess., 1949.

9. See *ibid., Hearings, on Housing and Urban Redevelopment*, p. 1559 and *passim*.

mercial facilities and at rents or prices within the financial means of the families displaced from the project area, decent, safe, and sanitary dwellings equal in number to the numbers of and available to such displaced families and reasonably accessible to their places of employment . . .[10]

On the surface, this statement seems to mark a significant advance from that which appeared in the public housing legislation of the 1930's. Clearly, it suggests a much greater concern for postrelocation needs. Yet lacking in this statute, as in the earlier one, is any explicit concern with the pressing social disruptions which are often caused or aggravated by relocation. This void, plus the lack of an adequate focus on housing in the redevelopment program, served to haunt renewal and relocation efforts throughout the 1950's, and to inhibit them greatly in the 1960's.

THE FIRST DECADE OF TITLE I

The 1949 Act led, within a very few years, to a substantial rise in the rate of residential displacement. In the face of a continuing housing shortage, which was even more oppressive for low-income urban households than for the population at large, redevelopment meant a further contraction in the housing supply. Not only did the displaced households have difficulty in finding decent units at moderate rents, but similar difficulties were felt throughout the low-income sector. Nor were the middle-class residents of areas adjacent to redevelopment sites entirely happy with the results. In many cities, alarmed denunciation of the "spread of slums" abounded.

Localities were hamstrung in their efforts to satisfy the principle of equivalent replacement that was implicit in the goal statement of the 1949 Housing Act. Unlike the situation under the earlier public housing program, rehousing was not an operative principle under urban renewal, in that no federal housing program was legislatively attached to the clearance phase of the process. Robert C. Weaver underscored the overriding importance of the housing supply when he said:

. . . relocation had been facilitated under the public housing program by the demand and supply relationship in the housing

10. U.S., *Statutes at Large*, LXIII, Part 1, 417.

> market. That relationship complicated the process as urban re-
> newal got under way. Regardless of how much effort might have
> been expended and how socially oriented it might have been, the
> sheer lack of vacancies in standard dwellings would have militated
> against a successful relocation program at that time.[11]

Simply put, low-cost housing units so badly needed in the early
1950's were just not being provided, and were in fact being withdrawn in the course of the redevelopment process. Even when
federal and local officials realized this inadequacy, they could do
little to meet the law's rehousing requirements. Relocation often
became an administrative obstacle to be hurdled or circumvented,
or at best, an opportunity to accomplish a minimum amount of
good for the people involved within the restraints imposed by the
political, social, and economic facts operative in each local instance.

Another imperfection in the housing market, that of racial discrimination, also militated against successful relocation. While a
number of renewal areas, particularly in New England, comprised
mostly whites, more and more projects were being undertaken in
Negro enclaves. Finding suitable homes for Negroes, especially if
they are poor or lacking in social skills, was and remains a difficult job indeed. Were it not for the governmental aids offered in
FHA and VA programs together with an enormous rise in real
income after the war, which permitted a vast suburban exodus of
whites and thereby opened up previously unavailable housing opportunities for nonwhites within the central cities, the problem
would have been considerably greater. Even as it was, however,
the in-migration of rural Southern Negroes continued to put pressure on the housing supply, and served to enlarge and consolidate
the ghetto. This in turn meant that renewal areas were more and
more likely to be Negro areas. To some Negroes in the North and
Midwest, relocation became almost a way of life.

A third impediment to successful relocation, aside from the
short supply of housing and racial discrimination in the market,
was the fact that the federal law had not foreseen the depth of
social problems that would be exposed by redevelopment, and that

11. Robert C. Weaver, *The Urban Complex* (Garden City, New York:
Doubleday, 1964), pp. 50-51.

at any rate the local agencies were not prepared to deal with these problems. Again, in Weaver's words:

> . . . the initial stages of public housing were initiated at a time when a large proportion of the American people were living in dilapidated and substandard housing. Those displaced by the program represented a large occupational, ethnic, age, and color cross-section of the nation. In more recent years, those displaced by urban renewal have been concentrated in lower-paid occupations and disproportionately composed of aged and minority groups. Consequently, in its initial stages urban renewal felt less effective political pressures to do a good job of relocation at the same time that the housing market complicated the process.[12]

PROGRESS AFTER MID-DECADE

Stimulated by both the desire to expedite redevelopment and the nation's interest in serving its low-income population, several new programs were initiated during and particularly near the end of the decade. Among the potentially important of these changes was the introduction of a number of new housing tools. These are discussed elsewhere in this volume, but a quick review here is in order as well.

As early as 1952, the Housing and Home Finance Agency, in one of its Local Public Agency (LPA) Letters,[13] advised the local agencies to make full use of the regional FHA offices in order to encourage builders to develop new housing for displaced families. In 1954, Congress made a concrete move toward easing rehousing problems by adding two new mortgage insurance sections to the National Housing Act. One was Section 221, which was designed to encourage the development of standard housing for relocatees outside the project area and to facilitate the purchase of existing housing by displaced persons through more fa-

---

12. *Ibid.,* p. 51.

13. Since February, 1951, HHFA and then HUD have periodically sent such letters to local public agencies in order to advise them of certain changes in program or emphasis, and to clarify certain policies or procedures. These letters, Congressional hearings, U.S. statutes, the Urban Renewal Manual, federal and state court decisions, relocation reports and studies, and interviews provide the bases of research for this chapter. For the LPA Letter referred to here, see *Local Public Agency Letter #8,* February 28, 1952.

vorable mortgage terms. Section 220, in contrast, aimed to assuage rehousing pressures primarily by rehabilitating deteriorated structures and conserving neighborhoods that might otherwise have had to be cleared and redeveloped.

The "220" and "221" programs, as amended, have resulted in benefits for some middle-income relocatees; but for the lower-income groups, who predominate in older areas, public housing, *per se,* has usually been the only road to decent housing. The 1949 Act had given relocatees a priority position on public housing waiting lists, and additional legislation during the decade reinforced this preferred status. Even had public housing restricted its service exclusively to relocatees, however, it could not have satisfied the need alone. As Charles E. Slusser pointed out in 1955:

. . . The size of the [public housing] program proposed in this bill is modest in relation to the needs of the families who are expected to be displaced by slum clearance and urban renewal activities and who will be eligible for admission to public housing. Because the incomes of those families are too low to find decent, safe, and sanitary dwellings offered by private enterprise, public housing must be provided for them before they can be displaced and their present slum dwellings be demolished. The provision of low-rent housing for these families is an absolute essential if the slum clearance and urban renewal program is to make the progress which is expected of it.[14]

By the middle of the decade, it had become quite clear that elderly relocatees constituted one of renewal's most aggrieved groups. In addition to the particularly severe physical and emotional discomforts that they endured upon displacement, they usually had considerable difficulty in getting mortgages for new homes or in finding suitable housing units to rent. The 1956 Housing Act took some cognizance of these problems by offering special privileges to older persons in securing public and private

14. U.S. Congress, Senate Subcommittee on Housing of the Committee on Banking and Currency, *Hearings, on Housing Amendments of 1955,* 84th Cong., 1st Sess., 1955, p. 73. Although the large-scale effort sought by Commissioner Slusser was not realized, a 1959 amendment tied public housing more closely to renewal by allowing localities to use certain expenditures for public housing built on renewal sites as noncash grant-in-aids credit toward their one-third share of renewal costs. Amendments in 1961 and 1964 made further concessions to the localities in regard to the land disposition price for public housing in renewal areas.

housing.[15] Single elderly persons were for the first time made eligible for admission to public housing, and extra federal subsidies were provided for the construction of public housing units designed for the aged. Income limits were modified, and the requirement that tenants come from substandard units was waived in the case of the elderly.

Some progress was also made, during the later part of the decade, in regard to private housing for the elderly. The 1956 Housing Act assisted older individuals in buying homes by authorizing the down payment to be made by a corporation or person other than the mortgagor when the latter is 60 years old or over. Another measure made nonprofit organizations eligible for FHA mortgage financing to build rental housing projects especially for the elderly. In the 1959 Housing Act, this program was broadened to include profit-making rental housing for the aged. Also in 1959, a program was initiated which provided for direct federal loans to promote rental housing for older persons. When implemented, such programs were often quite successful, but their magnitude was so small and their focus was so oriented around the middle and high-income elderly, that they became even less of a positive influence than the public housing program.

Of more direct value than the limited attempts to loosen the housing supply was the trend toward more liberal financial assistance for the relocatee. While the social and emotional needs of displaced families were also talked about, most of the action came in the realm of financial matters. Prior to 1956, only those who caused sufficient trouble or revealed extreme need had been granted any payments. But as a result of the 1956 Housing Act those displaced by renewal could receive ". . . reasonable and necessary moving expenses and any actual direct losses of property except goodwill or profit."[16] Individuals and families became eligible for a maximum payment of $100 and businesses for as much as $2000, all of which would be subsidized by the federal government. While the payments were minimal, and in many cases not adequate compensation for the real costs incurred or the

15. On November 8, 1956, HHFA issued *Local Public Agency Letter #82*, which was entitled "Relocation of the Elderly." It clarified the provisions of the 1956 Housing Act dealing with public and private housing for the elderly.

16. U.S., *Statutes at Large*, LXX, 1100-1101.

losses that were suffered, they did mark an important step. In the next three years, relocation payments were further increased and the rules governing them liberalized. Maximum allowable payments to business concerns were raised to $3000, while individuals and families became entitled to a maximum of $200 to cover their moving expenses and property losses. Concomitantly, policies were liberalized so that, by the end of the decade, relocation payments could be made in fixed amounts to individuals and families without the necessity of investigating the actual costs incurred in each case, and a temporary on-site move would no longer disqualify a relocatee for further relocation payments.

Probably the development with the greatest long-range effect on relocation was the emergence of the concept of comprehensive renewal planning, initiated in 1954 as the Workable Program and expanded in 1959 into the Community Renewal Program (CRP). Under these programs, the emphasis shifted from individual redevelopment projects to a communitywide attack on urban problems. As the focus of redevelopment broadened, relocation too was viewed in a broader light. Relocation was seen more as an opportunity, and less as an obstacle to desired changes in the use of urban land. Social welfare planning was discovered to be an essential part of urban redevelopment. The entire housing market was more likely to be considered than it had been under the earlier project orientation. Urban renewal was not viewed as an isolated phenomenon, but as part of a larger dynamic process.[17] In this context, HHFA dispatched an LPA letter advising local renewal agencies to coordinate their relocation activities with those of the highway program, and to provide referral services to

17. The legislation of the 1950's, however, was not altogether favorable for relocation, since urban redevelopment turned more conspicuously into a program designed to renew decaying central cities and drifted further away from the housing objective of the 1949 Act. While the 1949 law required that all redevelopment projects had to be predominantly residential either before or after redevelopment, amendments in 1954 and later years have allowed an increasing proportion of the urban renewal capital grant to be used for projects which were not predominantly residential after redevelopment.

An excellent review of the changes in the urban renewal program and its related components was prepared by Hilbert Fefferman of HUD. See U.S. Congress, Senate Subcommittee on Executive Reorganization of the Committee on Government Operations, *Hearings, Federal Role in Urban Affairs*, 89th Cong., 2nd Sess., 1966, pp. 40-78; see also Ashley A. Foard and Hilbert Fefferman, "Federal Urban Renewal Legislation," *Law and Contemporary Problems*, XXV (Winter, 1960), pp. 635-684.

persons displaced by highway activities on the same basis as those dislodged by renewal.[18] And, in 1959, Congress authorized relocation payments for all renewal area residents displaced by *any* type of governmental program.[19]

In practice, the Workable Program, the CRP, and related programs accomplished relatively little in the 1950's. Lacking the necessary resources, the communities in most instances were simply not yet capable of carrying out ambitious plans. The significance of these programs during the 1950's rests not on their concrete achievements, but rather on the sounder conceptual framework for urban planning. Indeed, in many respects they were the precursor of the Model Cities Program and of the important gains to be made in relocation in the 1960's.

Accompanying the greater governmental involvement in relocation was a growing intellectual interest in the matter. In its most practical form, this was evidenced in the many program reviews that accumulated during the decade.[20] By reporting the experience gained in local programs and illuminating the critical needs, these reviews surely had a role in guiding the direction of policy changes. Many of them, for instance, emphasized the need for financial assistance and for greater assistance to elderly persons and small businessmen.

Over and above their significance for the day-to-day operation of the relocation program, these reports contributed to a more sophisticated perspective on the redevelopment process itself. Among the methods discussed were a greater use of rehabilitation as opposed to rebuilding, a system of piecemeal clearance that would not require condemnation of entire renewal areas at one time, and the use of vacant sites for as much renewal as possible. Occasionally in these reports there was an indication that relocation had to be considered in a broader framework, and that standards of service ought to be raised substantially. In at least one

18. See *Local Public Agency Letter #103,* Sept. 12, 1957.

19. Let it be clear, however, that even by the end of the decade displaced nonrenewal area residents were not entitled by federal statute to any relocation payments or assistance.

20. See, for example: Chattanooga Housing Authority, *Relocation Plan,* 1952; New York City Housing Authority, *Report on Site Clearance and Relocation,* 1951; Detroit Housing Committee, Relocation Advisory Committee, *Displacement and Relocation in Detroit,* 1958; Chicago Plan Commission, *Population and Housing Report #2,* 1956; and Philadelphia Housing Association, *Relocation in Philadelphia,* 1958.

case, in fact, an attempt was made to develop a comprehensive plan involving physical, social, and economic elements for a specific population group (single males) residing in a single geographical area. Such positive approaches, though quite limited in number, pointed toward a distant horizon where relocation might be a ". . . positive urban renewal program rather than . . . an incidental activity appended to other programs, such as redevelopment, or housing code enforcement, as it is today."[21]

In terms of the knowledge gained by 1959, several common findings stand out in the relocation literature:

1. Public housing was absorbing a very small share of the relocation workload.
2. Most relocated families tended to relocate themselves and benefited only slightly from the relocation services provided.
3. Nonwhites typically relocated closer to the site, and were less dispersed in their relocation patterns than whites.
4. Housing costs were higher after relocation than before, although in some cases the higher prices were freely paid for superior accommodations.
5. Housing quality after relocation was generally at least as good as that which existed prior to the move.
6. Resentment was often voiced by individual residents and occasional reactions were voiced by groups of residents and organized opposition, particularly Negroes.
7. The more stable and deep-rooted occupants of the site, such as homeowners, the elderly, and small businessmen, suffered particular hardships.

When looking back upon these understandings, they leave large and obvious gaps. For one thing, the emphasis was still very much on housing, at the expense of more subtle (and possibly more important) matters. For another, although site offices had become fairly common, there was little attention given to the manner in which clients were treated or the skills needed to deal with them. For still another, little recognition was yet expressed concerning the overriding needs for service and assistance, independent of relocation *per se,* which have now become dominant themes in discussions of relocation. Thus, the limitations under which relocation operated were still accepted as given, and the program as

21. Howard W. Hallman, *A Study of Relocation in Philadelphia, 1955-1957* (Philadelphia: Philadelphia Housing Authority, 1959), p. 13.

well as the concept was still very much oriented around the mandate to "clear the site."

The advances that were made in relocation during the 1950's were influenced largely by the responsiveness of the concerned administrative officials to exposed needs and political pressures. By and large, the legislative branch played a comparatively passive—and often inhibiting—role, and the judicial branch stayed aloof of the issues altogether. In the classic Supreme Court case of *Berman v. Parker* and in subsequent lower court decisions, the rulings were predominantly in favor of redevelopment as expressed in law and elaborated in administrative procedures.[22] Thus, there was no effective "independent judgment" of redevelopment, and the rights of renewal area residents continued to be defined and redefined according to the experience and sensitivity of the practitioner more than by an appeal to principle or theory.

RECENT DEVELOPMENTS

A decade of experience with relocation under Title I and subsequent amendments of the 1949 Housing Act laid the basis for additional changes in the 1960's. The charge of relocation remained the same, but there evolved a pronounced sophistication in its operation and its social consciousness. By 1967, many agencies were providing such specialized relocation services as short-term family counseling, referral to appropriate social service agencies, health counseling, and training in homemaking and home management.

The most tangible legislative advance was in the financial assistance given to relocatees. In 1961 small businesses became eligible to receive full recompense for moving expenses, even if they were in excess of the previous limit of $3000;[23] nonprofit organizations were granted the same financial benefits as small businesses; and tenants whose rents rose by at least 10 percent as

22. See *Berman v. Parker,* 358, U.S. 269 (1954). Other notable cases are *Hunter v. City of New York,* 121 New York State 2nd 841 (1953); *Housing and Redevelopment Authority v. Minneapolis Metropolitan Co.,* 104 N.W. 2nd 864 (1960); *Gart v. Cole,* 166 Fed. Supp. 129 (1958); and *Barnes v. City of Gadsden,* 174 Fed. Supp. 64 (1958).

23. In 1962, HHFA imposed a $25,000 limit on allowable moving expenses, but this maximum has since been rescinded. See *Local Public Agency Letter #339,* Aug. 16, 1965.

a result of code enforcement or rehabilitation were deemed eligible for relocation payments. In 1964, even more substantial improvements were wrought, as Congressional hearings stressed the postrelocation financial hardships experienced by older individuals and small businesses. The housing legislation of that year entitled persons aged 62 years old or over to "relocation adjustment payments" up to $500[24] and made small businesses eligible for up to $1500 in excess of their moving costs to assist them in reestablishing their businesses. In 1965, the maximum allowance was raised to $2500, and more importantly, displaced property owners became eligible to recover certain settlement costs and related charges, such as transfer and recording fees. Small businessmen were further assisted in relocation when Congress made them eligible for low-interest loans through the Small Business Administration (SBA). HHFA cooperated by urging the local agencies to make full use of the regional SBA offices, which offer counseling as well as credit assistance.

Limited strides were also made in the early 1960's in enlarging the supply of adequate rehousing. The new "221 (d) (3)" program, for example, was initiated in 1961 as a measure to provide more moderate rentals through below-market interest rates for developers. Public housing projects designed exclusively for older persons became quite popular. In 1965, a rent supplement program, involving private enterprise, was enacted in an effort to widen the range of new housing which displaced persons and other persons of modest means could afford. In the same year, local housing authorities were encouraged to develop their own imaginative means of providing low-cost housing. Finally, a 1966 amendment to the urban renewal law required that every urban renewal area intended primarily for residential use contain "a substantial number of units of standard housing of low and moderate cost and result in marked progress in serving the poor and disadvantaged. . . ."[25] These programs, along with a general

24. Such payments, however, were excluded in the case of those persons who relocated in low-rent housing projects.

25. U.S. Congress, House, *Demonstration Cities and Metropolitan Development Act of 1966,* 89th Cong., 2nd Sess., 1966, Report No. 2301, p. 28. This requirement, it should be understood, applies only to those projects which are primarily residential upon redevelopment. In those projects which are primarily nonresidential upon redevelopment but in which a

loosening in the housing market in the late 1950's and early 1960's and somewhat stricter code enforcement, served to brighten the chances that displaced persons would find adequate housing, especially in contrast to the prospects they faced in the early 1950's. Yet due to the lack of adequate funding, the impact of these programs has thus far been minimal.

Accompanying these policy changes were improvements in actual administration and local performances. At the federal level, the Urban Renewal Administration ". . . established higher minimum standards, provided for more frequent field inspections and more stringent review of relocation plans and progress reports, and upgraded the quality of local statistics submitted by local public agencies executing programs."[26] At the local level, better cooperation was secured from housing agencies, particularly public housing. A number of centralized relocation agencies were begun, and a few of these were given auspices over virtually all relocation regardless of its cause. The relocation process was streamlined in many respects, and local offices became much more responsive to clients' needs. Relocation planning was more likely to begin at an early date in the redevelopment process; personnel standards were improved; the cost of coordination of social service activities and diagnostic surveys became allowable local expenses; and follow-up procedures were strengthened.

In reviewing these developments, it is obvious that a greater effort was made to come to grips with the social problems imposed by relocation. While relocation in the early 1950's was seldom viewed outside its housing context, it has in recent years been considered also in terms of neighborhood familiarity, friendships, convenience and other social factors that are affected by displacement. On the national level, three Congressional subcommittees have held hearings since 1961 specifically exploring these mat-

---

substantial number of persons are nevertheless displaced, there is no such explicit statement that appropriate housing and assistance to the poor must be provided. Thus, localities can still circumvent the requirement quoted above by simply embarking upon projects that are predominantly nonresidential, but such a tendency has been partially frustrated by recent administrative directives that effectively focus local renewal programs now being planned on the needs of low-income households. See *Local Public Agency Letter #418,* May 19, 1967.

26. Weaver, *op. cit.,* pp. 105-106.

ters,[27] and in 1964, President Johnson officially acknowledged their importance by noting to Congress that ". . . the human cost of relocation remains a serious and difficult problem."[28]

Two recent advances, which have not yet been fully realized, deserve a degree of close attention. One has to do with the timing and intensity of relocation assistance. It has become abundantly clear that the withholding of relocation services until the last minute brings on confusion, panic, and general opposition on the part of many residents, and that by the time relocation services are actually provided, the area is likely to have become a most undesirable place to live as the inhabitants gradually leave and maintenance is virtually abandoned. To minimize these possibilities, the housing legislation of 1964 called for the formation of relocation assistance programs in renewal areas at the earliest possible time. Congress envisioned these programs as serving the threefold purpose of determining the needs of those to be displaced, of providing information and help, and of promoting the coordination of relocation activities. In the meantime, some local agencies have adopted the procedure of granting relocation payments to households who desire to move even during the planning stage. This practice involves no direct cost to the locality as long as the area is in fact redeveloped, since the moving costs are eventually reimbursed by the federal government.

A second current advance has to do with the uniformity and adequacy of relocation payments. The development of a community-wide perspective on relocation, which was first formalized in the Workable Program and further elaborated in the Community Renewal Program, led rather quickly to the notion that the administration of all relocation activity, regardless of its source, should be unified at the local level. Indeed, by 1964, this realization made its way into the Housing Act which called for ". . . the coordination of relocation activities and other planned or pro-

27. See U.S. Congress, Senate, Special Committee on Aging, *Hearings, before the Subcommittee on Involuntary Relocation of the Elderly,* 87th Cong., 2nd Sess., 1962; Committee on Public Works, *Hearings, before the Select Subcommittee on Real Property Acquisition,* 1964; and U.S. Congress, House, Select Committee on Small Business, *Hearings, before Subcommittee No. 5,* 89th Cong., 1st Sess., 1965.

28. This quote is taken from *Message from the President of the United States, Relative to Drafts of Bills Relating to Housing,* June 27, 1964, p. 5.

posed governmental actions in the community which may affect the carrying out of the relocation program."[29]

A community-wide perspective also brought to the fore the need for uniform relocation rights. The disparities in relocation payments and other assistance available to persons displaced by different governmental programs became all too clear. A small businessman displaced by urban renewal might, for example, receive as much as $25,000 or more to cover moving expenses while his counterpart displaced by highway construction would be entitled to only $3000 or possibly less. The unequal treatment of persons in equal circumstances soon became obvious. What is more, it distorted the image of the urban renewal program, which had moved much farther toward positive relocation services than had the other programs, but which continued to be identified with the sins of its brothers.

In 1962, Congress for the first time made those persons displaced by the highway program eligible for relocation payments, and, in 1964, it provided public housing relocatees with the same benefits enjoyed by urban renewal relocatees. Legislation in 1965 and, most recently in 1966, further extended these benefits to cover virtually all programs under the aegis of the new Department of Housing and Urban Development, and the Demonstration Cities and Metropolitan Development Act of 1966 applied the same relocation standards to Model Cities programs that are used in urban renewal.

In 1965, the Advisory Commission on Intergovernmental Relations issued a report on the unequal treatment of relocatees, and gave its prestigious support to uniform relocation legislation.[30] Largely as a result of the Commission's study, a number of bills have now been introduced in Congress to promote uniform benefits for all persons displaced by federally assisted programs. The most notable of these, S. 1681, was sponsored by Senators Muskie and Javits, and was a broad-based bill encompassing: (1) relocation payments, (2) advisory assistance, (3) assurance of availability of standard housing, (4) federal reimbursement for relocation

29. U.S., *Statutes at Large*, LXXVIII, 786.

30. See Advisory Commission on Intergovernmental Relations, *Relocation: Unequal Treatment of People and Businesses Displaced by Governments*, January, 1965.

payment under federally assisted programs, and (5) certain land acquisition practices.[31] This bill, introduced in 1966, passed the Senate but met with resistance in the House of Representatives and eventually died in committee. Its major provisions, however, were reintroduced in the 90th Congress, in the Intergovernmental Cooperation Act of 1967, S. 698. Under the proposed legislation, small businessmen displaced by programs involving the federal government could receive up to $5000, whether or not they reestablished, in addition to full recompense for moving expenses; and displaced households, depending on certain criteria, could receive as much as $200 for moving expenses, $100 as a dislocation allowance, $300 toward the purchase of a new home, and $1000 in rental subsidies for a two-year period with the federal government paying the difference between 20 percent of a household's income and the rental cost of a dwelling of "modest" standards. Thus, not only does the measure offer uniform benefits, but it also represents a long-sought improvement in financial benefits to those in greatest need.

REFLECTIONS ON THE CURRENT SITUATION

Intensive research into relocation is still a rarity, and local reports are often superficial or apologetic in nature, but some scholarly reports have appeared in recent years. Among the most outstanding of these are works by Elizabeth Wood, Herbert Gans, and Chester Hartman,[32] which have increasingly questioned whether renewal has perhaps put the cart before the horse. In Gans' words, "The relocation plan should take priority over the renewal phase of the total plan, and no renewal plans should be approved by federal or local agencies until a proper relocation plan has been developed."[33]

The academic community, however, has on the whole had little

31. U.S. Congress, Senate, *Uniform Relocation Act of 1966,* 89th Cong., 2nd Sess., 1966, Report 1378, p. 1.

32. See Elizabeth Wood, *A Report Concerning Certain Aspects of Relocation,* A Report Prepared for the Office of the Development Coordinator, Philadelphia, 1961; Herbert J. Gans, "The Human Implication of Current Redevelopment and Relocation Planning," *Journal of the American Institute of Planners* (February, 1959); and Chester Hartman, "The Housing of Relocated Families," *Journal of the American Institute of Planners* (November, 1964).

33. Gans, *ibid.,* p. 20. Although his article appeared in the 1950's, we can consider Gans at least a few years ahead of his time.

to do with the changes in relocation policy and philosophy. Experience has in this case been the teacher, and learning has thus been quite incremental and unsystematic. What is more, the apparent increasing degree of success in relocation has been due to exogenous factors as much as to changes within the operation of the program itself. The housing market, for example, has loosened a bit in many cities; the political climate became more sympathetic, at least until very recent years; and the welfare community in most cities has become more responsive. All these conditions have made relocation an easier task to perform than it was at the outset of the urban renewal program.

Whether relocation can continue to improve is also contingent on factors beyond the present control of relocation officials. The most crucial among these is discrimination in the housing market. In the face of a paucity of effective desegregation policies and compounded by the dearth of suitable low-income housing in general, relocation is likely to operate for some time to come within a segregated and highly restricted housing market. This means that relocation officials are and will continue to be restrained in satisfactorily rehousing a large proportion of their clients.

We seem to have reached a juncture where relocation as it is presently constituted, and when at its best, has adopted most of the basic improvements that are possible within its general purview. To be sure, marginal improvements can still be made. Among other things, financial benefits can be raised, social services can be expanded, and all relocation programs can be made uniform. With a few more improvements it can perform its secondary task of facilitating redevelopment reasonably well and at the same time provide some small measure of comfort to the displaced. But even with these improvements, relocation will remain largely a set of procedures to be followed, in a relatively uninfluential area of public activity.

On the other hand, were the program reconstituted and elevated to a position of priority importance in the redevelopment process, it might readily be turned into a more positive program, designed primarily to provide real opportunity to the urban poor, and only secondarily to serve some other public purpose. That it is possible to think in terms of this second alternative is in itself indicative of the substantial advance the relocation program has made since its beginnings thirty years ago.

3

CHAPTER

THE CONDITION OF THE ELDERLY
IN URBAN AMERICA[1]

Throughout modern history, the aging process has been viewed by poets, playwrights, and philosophers as an enigma. Some have stressed the compensations of age; others, the penalties. The only agreement seems to be that aging is a vast and complex process, and that to age successfully takes a great deal of skill. La Rochefoucauld offered the simple maxim: "Few people know how to grow old." Amiel expressed it in these terms: "To know how to grow old is the masterwork of wisdom and one of the most difficult chapters in the art of living."

Recent, more "scientific" efforts to understand aging have further exposed its complexities, but a basic mystery still exists as to its nature. These inquiries have led to two contrasting theories, each of which is widely held. The dominant one, and the one that seems to agree with the layman's attitude, is that people are happiest when they feel useful and that the elderly should therefore adopt roles that allow them to participate fully in the life of the society. A person is described as "well adjusted" if he remains as active as he was during his middle years, and as "maladjusted" to the extent that he becomes less active.[2]

The other view of aging takes a quite different position. Here,

1. Much of the material in this chapter relies on an earlier publication by Paul L. Niebanck, entitled *The Elderly in Older Urban Areas: Problems of Adaptation and the Effects of Relocation* (Institute for Environmental Studies, University of Pennsylvania, 1965). See the primary source for more detailed findings and a comprehensive bibliography.

2. Much of this is summarized in Arnold Rose, "A Current Theoretical Issue in Social Gerontology," *The Gerontologist,* Vol. 4, No. 1 (March, 1964), pp. 46-50.

successful adaptation to old age is regarded as a process of gradual disengagement, commensurate with one's declining capacities and eventual death.[3] The performance of useful roles is not a valued objective, and attempts to remain active are felt to inhibit a satisfactory adjustment. Supporters of this theory point to studies which show that morale is higher among eighty-year-olds than among those in their seventies. They conclude that the happier "very old" persons become content with their status only after making the disengaging adjustments necessary in their sixties and seventies.

Both of these theories have been extensively criticized, but no thoroughgoing alternative or synthesis has yet been produced.[4] We are left with the thought that successful aging may be more a function of individual personalities and experiences than of a universally applicable theory. The fact remains, in any case, that a great many adjustments must be made in the course of growing old, and that these adjustments are more difficult under some circumstances than under others.

Adapting oneself to old age has been said to be more difficult in the United States, where the elderly are typically ignored or even looked down upon, than in many other parts of the world, where age is more likely to be regarded as a sign of honor and authority.[5] The comparative neglect of the older person in this country seems to stem from the high value that is generally placed on economic productivity and social leadership. In these terms, the elderly have comparatively little to offer, and as a result they are often rejected by the society as a whole and tend to withdraw to more passive roles than those which would otherwise be normal.

The problems of the elderly have not gone wholly without attention, however, and in recent years a number of important programs have been instituted to assist them in meeting their needs. It is on these kinds of programs that the elderly relocatee must

3. See Elaine Cumming and William Henry, *Growing Old: The Process of Disengagement* (New York: Basic Books, 1961).

4. Bernard Kutner is one of the pioneers in this field. He terms the aging process as one of redifferentiation or reintegration of functions, leading eventually to stabilization. See his treatment, "The Social Nature of Aging," *The Gerontologist*, Vol. 2, No. 1 (March, 1962), p. 8.

5. See Irving Rosow, "Old Age: One Moral Dilemma of an Affluent Society," *The Gerontologist*, Vol. 2, No. 4 (December, 1962).

rely for necessary assistance, beyond that offered by the relocation program itself. The present chapter is intended to provide understanding of the nature and depth of the problems faced by such persons, and the extent to which they are equipped with the personal and institutional resources necessary to meet the challenge of relocation.

INCOME

The recent notice that has been given to poverty in our society has revealed that large segments of our aged population are totally without economic freedom, and many others are severely restricted. Rural poverty has been with us for many generations, but urban poverty among the elderly, which in qualitative terms often has harsher consequences than rural poverty, has now reached numerical ascendance as well. For the elderly residents of the inner urban areas that are subject to clearance and redevelopment, poverty is usually endemic (Table 1).

TABLE 1	Income Distribution of Elderly Households, Cities and Relocation Workloads Compared				
	Percent of households with annual incomes of less than				
	$1000	$2000	$3000	$4000	$5000
Two-or-more person households					
Cities as a whole	8	20	31	40	50
Relocation populations	10	41	59	72	83
One-person households					
Cities as a whole	37	64	76	83	89
Relocation populations	42	82	90	95	98

Source: Unweighted averages of experience in five cities, as detailed in Niebanck, *op. cit.,* p. 18.

The incomes of most elderly city-dwellers are not only low, but often subject to further decline. Poor health, obsolescent skills, and other handicaps usually mean early retirement. Part-time work or income from savings is hardly sufficient to replace even the meager wages to which these people were accustomed in their younger years. Pensions are rare, and even Social Security is not always available. In one poverty-stricken area of San Antonio, for example, many retired elderly persons were discovered to be ineligible for Social Security because they had worked for individuals rather than for companies, and many were also without income from private pensions because they had worked intermittently, or for companies that provided no such benefits.[6] Public assistance, in such instances, was their only source of support, and for some even this was not available because of highly restrictive citizenship requirements.

To sustain themselves under conditions of low and declining income, the elderly must, as a rule, make drastic and undesirable adjustments in their spending patterns. Having barely enough even for their most pressing needs, these persons are denied many of the small, but sustaining, comforts. Expenditures for transportation, tobacco, small gifts, occasional entertainment, or even church services are often far beyond their means. Such items are important to the dignity of any individual, especially an elderly person who suddenly finds his personal worth being challenged on many sides. The plight of an elderly woman interviewed in Providence is illustrative:

"I go as far as six dollars a month will take me. I watch my pennies and save up for what I need. It would be nice if the elderly could get a raise to get what we need—like stockings and slippers and a dress. Either you get the clothes you need or you use the money to have a change by seeing the stores and having lunch downtown with a friend."

For many older persons, it is not only the comforts of life that are prohibitively expensive, but many of the basic necessities as well. Comparing actual incomes with Bureau of Labor Statistics standards, fully half of the elderly households in renewal areas are financially unable to achieve a "modest but adequate" level of living, and many of these are in the deepest of financial distress. This is particularly true as age advances, and it is more true for nonwhites than for whites and for small families than for large. Thus, an urban dweller who is very old, of minority status, a woman, and living alone, is especially likely to suffer from low, or

6. The cases cited herein are taken from the reports of the four demonstration projects associated with this study. For a fuller description, see Chapter 4.

greatly reduced, income. At the extreme, a Negro female, living alone, of age 75 or older, is likely to have only about two dollars a day available for all her needs (Table 2).

TABLE 2	Proportions of Elderly Households in Potential Renewal Areas Having Inadequate Incomes, by Race, Age, and Family Type					
	Head Aged 60-64		Head Aged 65-74		Head Aged 75 or Older	
	White	Nonwhite	White	Nonwhite	White	Nonwhite
Percent of two-or-more-person households with incomes under $2000	19	33	35	57	44	52
Percent of male one-person households with incomes under $1000	26	39	34	46	44	52
Percent of female one-person households with incomes under $1000	36	57	49	62	61	75

Source: Medians for seven cities providing data from their relocation workloads, as reported in Niebanck, *op. cit.*, p. 27.

Sources of Income

The income for the elderly population as a whole is derived primarily from present or past earnings, as might be expected. For all persons in the United States aged 65 or over taken together, 32 percent of their current income is the result of job earnings, 15 percent comes from personal investments, 30 percent from Social Security, 9 percent from retirement programs, and only 5 percent from the public sector (from funds to which recipients have not directly contributed).[7] Logically enough, those having the narrowest range of income sources live in renewal areas. Single persons and members of minority groups, both of which are overrepresented in the older areas, often depend on very few or only one

7. See Committee on Education and Labor, House of Representatives, 88th Cong., 2nd Sess., *Poverty in the U.S.* (Washington, D.C.: USGPO, April, 1964) and Lenore Epstein, "Income of the Aged in 1962: First Findings of the 1963 Survey of the Aged," *Social Security Bulletin,* Vol. 27, No. 3 (March, 1964), Table 4, p. 53.

means of income. Most commonly, that source is Social Security. Others, unfortunately, are almost totally dependent on public support. In the demonstration project area studied in San Francisco, for example, public assistance is the largest single source of income.

Occupational Status

As might be expected, considerable numbers of persons just beyond normal retirement age continue to participate actively in the labor force, but this proportion declines sharply as age progresses. Older people who do continue to work are found, in disproportionately large numbers, in industries and occupations requiring fairly high levels of skill, experience, or education. The jobs that require lesser degrees of achievement, on the other hand, tend to go to younger persons, who have a competitive advantage over their elders.

As a result of these tendencies, the older residents of central urban areas are less likely to be employed than older persons elsewhere. Their comparatively low skills place them among the most dispensable of employees. Furthermore, among those who do work, wages are often exceedingly low. Employment, then, is hardly a fruitful means to a decent income for most of these persons, even though they are many times in desperate need of additional money and are willing to work in order to get it.

Income Maintenance Programs

The dependence of many older residents of central cities on public income maintenance programs is exacerbated by the fact that most of these programs are wholly inadequate to the task.[8] Old Age Assistance (OAA) grants, for example, which are received by two million persons, are incredibly low in all except a few states. To receive as much as $90 each month under OAA in the state of Texas, for example, is so rare as to be almost nonexistent. In more than half of all the states, even the maximum allowable grants, to say nothing of the average grants, fail to meet the minimum standards of financial need defined by the state welfare departments themselves, and fall far short of the levels of ade-

8. See, among many other sources, Welfare Administration, "Programs and Operating Statistics," *Welfare in Review,* Vol. 2, No. 5 (May, 1964).

quacy established by the Bureau of Labor Statistics and other agencies concerned with the elimination of poverty.[9]

Besides the severe limitations on allowable grants as established by the individual states, the OAA program suffers from many other inadequacies. One of these has to do with the nature of the means tests that determine eligibility. In addition to being an affront to the applicant's privacy and dignity, they are often unrealistically exclusive. Indicative of this is the case of the indigent New York couple who, in order to qualify for aid, had to sell its prized heirlooms, the possession of which put its assets just above the stringent maximum allowable. Recent federal amendments have been designed to liberalize many such restrictions, but few states have as yet taken advantage of the changes, even though their share of the total cost would be extremely small.

The other major income maintenance program, Old Age Survivors and Disability Insurance (OASDI), is not subject to many of the criticisms justly aimed at public assistance. Its standards of support are consistent from state to state and, while not altogether adequate in many cases, are nevertheless more responsive to changes in actual need. Furthermore, receipt of Social Security benefits is not contingent on a means test, and there is no social stigma associated with this kind of program.

Social Security is not above reproach, however. Its coverage, although recently extended, is still not universal and payments to certain classes of the population, particularly the widow, are pathetically low. Another weakness in the program stems from one of its original goals, which was to encourage the elderly to withdraw from the labor force. If a person desires to supplement his income by working, he is often subject to a penalty in the form of a reduction in his Social Security payment. These weaknesses in the program still cause difficulty for older persons living in redevelopment areas and other older urban areas, who, as was noted above, are likely to be quite dependent on these public programs.

Prospects for Improvement

If the income status of the impoverished urban elderly population is to be improved, in the short run, it will clearly have to be

9. For dated but relevant statistics here, see U.S. Department of Health, Education, and Welfare: *Characteristics of State Public Assistance Plans Under the Social Security Act; General Provisions* (Washington, D.C.: USGPO, 1960).

through governmental initiative. To accelerate the changes that are necessary, the elderly must make effective use of their potential political power. Fortunately, they have shown signs recently of becoming a more potent political power. They have, for instance, evinced a higher voting rate than the young.[10] Studies have shown that more than 80 percent of the eligible voters in their sixties actually vote. Moreover, several elderly interest groups have been formed, outstanding among which are the National Council of Senior Citizens, the American Association of Retired Persons, the National Retired Teachers Association, and the National Association of Retired Civil Employees.

Optimism is thus warranted, at least at the federal level. In 1965, Congress passed the Older Americans Act, which established an Administration on Aging within the Department of Health, Education, and Welfare. It serves as a clearinghouse on problems of the elderly and a source of programs designed to advance a broad set of goals. While the eventual impact of the new agency is still uncertain, it does mark a step which appears to be in a forward direction. The passage of the "Medicare" and "Medicaid" programs and the continuing expansion of Social Security benefits will, in combination, do much to bring the real incomes of elderly persons into conformity with modern standards of living. Barring any pronounced change in the national political climate, then, the outlook for greater federal assistance to the aged is bright. Even the more far-reaching legislative changes are not altogether favorable to the urban elderly, however. The proposed changes in the Social Security law are in many ways regressive, for example, and thereby offer the poor comparatively less than they offer the financially secure. Whether the urban elderly population will benefit in fair proportion to the other sectors of the elderly group, then, remains a moot question.

Relocation's Impact on Income

In the demonstration projects associated with this study, no significant changes in income before and after relocation were observed. Other inquiries, however, have noted a considerably more severe

10. Angus Campbell, "Social and Psychological Determinants of Voting Behavior," in *Politics of Age,* C. Tibbitts and W. Donahue, Eds. Proceedings of the 14th Annual Conference on Aging, Ann Arbor: University of Michigan, June 19-20, 1961, p. 91.

impact. Of fifty displaced elderly households interviewed for this study in Philadelphia, one-third experienced a loss in income, while only two individuals experienced a gain. Similarly, a study of 69 elderly families displaced from an ethnic, working class section of Boston found that nearly one-half of the families suffered a decline in their incomes.[11] In most of these instances, the loss of rental income, small businesses, or local jobs explained the financial setback.

Particularly severe is the financial and emotional hardship felt by the displaced, elderly small businessmen. Most of us have had some contact with a long-established "Ma and Pa" type of neighborhood store, whose trade depends upon a local, familiar clientele. Although these businesses provide only marginal incomes, the recompense is usually far superior than that which would be received upon retirement, especially since few of the elderly owners are eligible for Social Security benefits. To relocate such a business is a financial and physical burden usually beyond the means of an older person. Reestablishment means that a new location must be found, equipment must be moved, new equipment must be purchased, a new clientele must be developed, and legal fees must be paid. Most older small businessmen will retire rather than submit to this ordeal.

Overall, the economic impact of relocation on older persons is two-edged. On the one hand, there is the direct financial loss experienced by many. On the other, there is the more indirect reversal occasioned by higher expenses in the new location. Of the latter, the most oppressive is the increased costs of housing usually experienced after displacement. In three cities for which data were available for this study, rents paid by multiperson elderly households rose by an overall average of more than 10 percent and for one-person households, by almost 20 percent (Table 3). Similarly, a Housing and Home Finance Agency-Bureau of the Census study in 1963, which included a representative sample of households (of all ages) displaced by renewal projects, found that median rents increased by 12 percent after relocation.[12]

---

11. United Community Services of Metropolitan Boston, *Housing Preferences of Older People* (Boston: United Community Services, January, 1962), p. 13.

12. Housing and Home Finance Agency, *The Housing of Relocated Families,* Washington, D.C., March, 1965.

TABLE 3	Changes in Rent, for Elderly Households Who Rented Both Before and After Relocation	
Types of change	Two-or-more-person households	One-person households
Total	100%	100%
Increase of $25 or more	15	12
Increase of $15 to $24	17	19
Increase of $5 to $14	25	22
Approximately constant	16	30
Decrease of $5 to $14	16	12
Decrease of $15 or more	11	5
Median rent, before moving	$48	$37
Median rent, after moving	$55	$44

Source: Composite of sample data received from relocation agencies in three cities, as reported in Niebanck, *op. cit.*, p. 131.

Along with increased housing costs, the relocated elderly are often beset with greater expenses for transportation, food, and other essentials. The loss of a close personal relationship with the neighborhood grocer may, for example, lead to more expensive delivery costs or make short-term credit less accessible. The cumulative effect of such factors can make the financial situation after relocation considerably more difficult than before.

At present, little is done to help elderly persons maintain or improve their postrelocation incomes. Those displaced by urban renewal and public housing programs do receive moving expenses and payments for related expenditures, but even for them, the financial benefit is a short-term one. For example, an elderly small businessman forced to retire by an urban renewal project is not entitled to a special pension or any other such compensation which can promote long-term security. At best, social caseworkers might help him secure increased Old Age Assistance or Social Security benefits along with his relocation payments. Yet even in these cases, elderly relocatees must contend with direct or indirect financial losses and must, on their own, make the difficult budget adjustments.

HOUSING

As with their income, the housing situation of elderly persons living in older urban areas is generally quite inadequate. For one thing, the structural condition of these housing units is frequently very poor. While the housing of most elderly households, as measured by the Bureau of the Census, is not strikingly bad, in older areas the extent of poor housing is unquestionably great. Furthermore, when size, location, safety, and environmental factors are taken into account, virtually all of the low-income elderly residents of older areas are inappropriately housed in one important respect or another.

Part of the difficulty, of course, is the age and obsolescence of the housing units themselves. Older people, as a rule, live in older housing, and in central areas this condition applies almost universally. Low value and rent levels also contribute to poor quality, in that they limit the amount of money available to maintain or improve the properties. The physical weakness and limited expectations of the people themselves also have a bearing on the condition of these properties. Finally, many older areas are so neglected and impoverished in ways other than housing quality *per se,* that they discourage whatever impulses toward improvement might exist even among the comparatively well-to-do.

Despite the fact that the housing and environmental conditions in older areas are often in conflict with, and usually inappropriate to, the needs of the elderly, such areas do have important compensations. They provide services and facilities which may not be available, or are less conveniently available, in sections of the city further removed from downtown. Social ties with both individuals and institutions in the area may be great. Housing costs, as was said, are quite low (Table 4). In fact, these older areas are often the only neighborhoods in which the elderly can live without sacrificing other necessary consumption items in order to pay their housing bills. The savings in housing costs are particularly impor-

TABLE 4	Monthly Housing Costs of Elderly Renters, for Cities and Relocation Workloads				
	Percent of households paying less than				
	$30	$40	$50	$60	$80
Cities as a whole	9	18	30	43	69
Relocation populations	33	52	73	84	96

Source: Unweighted averages of experience in seven cities, as detailed in Niebanck, *op. cit.,* p. 57.

tant to homeowners,[13] who are very common among the elderly residents of declining areas. Many elderly owners are free of mortgage debt, and the taxes on their properties are likely to be very low. In the absence of a necessity to "keep up with Joneses," even outlays for maintenance and repair can be postponed to an indefinite future date. Besides these savings, home ownership has important psychological value, and is a symbol of security and independence.

A correlative to the extent of home ownership is the residential stability of the inner-city elderly population. It is commonly believed that older areas are occupied by people who are accustomed to moving, but among the elderly, this view is not substantiated in fact. In one of the cities that was subjected to analysis in the course of this study, for example, it was found that two-thirds of the elderly cases on the relocation workload had lived at the same address for ten years or more.

Residential stability cannot necessarily be taken as a sign of residential satisfaction, however. As one grows older, one's needs for space change, important relationships to the physical and social environment are altered or severed, and underlying tastes often shift. There is no question, therefore, that relocation can serve to improve the living conditions of the elderly, in both objective and subjective ways. Opportunities to change one's tenure, or location, or even simply the size or style of the abode, are often welcomed by the displaced households.

Each household thus has its own particular needs for living space, but often of even more importance are its needs for proximity to facilities and services and for the establishment of supportive human relationships. Involuntary relocation must be accompanied by a certain amount of gentle persuasion and assurance that financial and other losses will not be so powerful as to negate the benefits that relocation does provide. Furthermore, public relocation programs must go much farther toward determining just what combination of housing and environmental fac-

13. While home ownership is realistically not as common in areas susceptible to renewal as it is in more outlying areas, roughly half of all elderly households of two or more members were found to have owned their homes prior to relocation in a sample of five cities. Even among one-person households, about one out of every five owned their own homes prior to relocation.

tors are best suited to each client, and they must make more of an effort to reproduce or at least compensate for the positive elements of the old neighborhood.

Housing Programs for the Elderly

The housing needs of older persons have not gone wholly without public recognition, and a number of programs have been initiated, some very sensitive to the specific needs of the elderly and others of a more general nature. Public housing is of course the most active and the first of the programs to pay attention to the needs of the elderly in central cities. Prior to 1962, even public housing had few special provisions for the elderly, but since that year almost half of all new units have been designed and set aside specifically for them. Many relocatees, including single persons and members of deprived minority groups, have benefited greatly by the change in public housing policy. There is a large demand for good public housing, among both the moderately poor, whom the program does serve, and the abject poor, whom the program has not thus far served. A great expansion in public housing for older citizens seems to be in order, in view of the fact that this single program is carrying the majority of the burden for assisting the urban elderly, and because even its efforts have gone only a small distance, perhaps 10 percent at the very most, toward satisfying the need that exists.

Another housing resource for the aged is the so-called "202" direct loan program. Initiated by the Housing Act of 1959 to provide homes for those senior citizens whose incomes are too high for public housing but too low to pay for suitable housing in the private market, the "202" program offers direct loans on favorable terms to nonprofit corporations, cooperatives, and others who have an interest in providing housing for older Americans. The scope of the "202" program is as yet too limited to have a widespread impact on the housing needs of the elderly. Its major drawback, however, is not its current size, but the fact that it leaves out a large number of households with incomes between about $2000 and $3000. These families are neither served adequately by public housing nor able to pay the rents required in most "202" projects. Moreover, the unexpectedly high costs of construction of many "202" projects has resulted in inordinately high rents even for occupants who otherwise could hardly be considered poor.

Many programs originally administered by the Federal Housing Administration (FHA) are also designed to benefit the elderly, either directly or indirectly. Two of the more prominent of these are "231" and "232." The "231" program provides mortgage insurance for both profit and nonprofit groups for the construction of new multifamily rental housing for the elderly. The rent levels for these projects, however, are even higher than for those under "202." Only a small fraction have monthly rents under $80, thereby putting them well beyond the means of most older city folk. The "232" program, which allows 90 percent mortgage guarantees for the construction of nursing homes, is, in effect, more of a health resource than a housing resource. Principally because of its profitability, this program has rapidly become popular.

Potentially one of the most effective programs is contained in Section 221 (d) (3) of the 1961 Housing Act. While not a direct loan program, "221 (d) (3)" is similar to "202" in that it results in mortgages to limited dividend corporations, but in this instance the insurance can be provided for rehabilitation as well as new construction. It is, however, limited to multiunit developments and is designed to help families in the "middle-income" range. Although it has not yet lived up to its potential, this program seems destined to take its place with "202" as a valuable aid for the elderly who receive incomes above the average for their age group but below the average for the population as a whole. Furthermore, it might add significantly to the array of tools designed to help the poor, if the rent supplement program to which "221 (d) (3)" is allied is allowed to expand.

The rent supplementation program, which has enormous theoretical possibilities but has already aroused resistance and controversy, is one of three emerging federal programs that could be of substantial help to the urban elderly. The potential of the rent supplement mechanism will be discussed shortly. The second of these innovations, just getting under way, involves financial grants to low-income residents of renewal areas to make it possible for them to improve their properties to acceptable minimum standards. The advantage here is that the familiar environment, including its institutions and much of its population, is not disturbed, but the housing can be dramatically improved. The third program, already being employed in a few cities, allows public housing authorities to acquire or lease structures of varying types in scattered locations, so as to assure the widest possible range of choice to low-income households. Again, for the elderly as well as for others, the possibilities here are enormous.

An Assessment of the Situation

Although the existing housing programs serving the elderly have had a very limited overall impact to date, they still provide a worthy basis for future efforts. In recent years, the programs have shown a genuine "consumer-orientation" and have been innovative and sensitive to the particular housing and locational needs of older persons. To reach those households in greatest need, however, they need additional tools to counteract the excessive land, construction, and administration costs which have served to inflate rents.

A fully implemented system of rent supplements, applied to public housing as well as to "202," "231," and "221 (d) (3)" housing, would make these programs particularly valuable to elderly relocatees. Even a modest supplement would bring the federally assisted private developments within the range of the rent-paying ability of many elderly relocatees. In fact, it is estimated that an average supplement of only twenty dollars a month would more than double the "effective demand" for assisted and publicly constructed units at the time of relocation (Table 5). A supplement of more substantial size would, of course, go a long way toward making the market more responsive to the needs of the relocatee and others like him. Without some such income or rent mechanism, however, the potential of the current programs in serving low-income elderly households can hardly be realized.

Relocation and Housing

While it is necessary to treat the needs of each elderly household as a unique case, certain general guidelines can be drawn to help plan for their rehousing. It has been found that among the things that become important as old age approaches are:

1. *Modified independence.* Self-direction is cherished, in view of

TABLE 5	Estimated Annual Response of Displaced Elderly Households to a Modest Program of Rent Supplementation	
	Approximate number of relocated elderly households served each year by public housing, "202," "231," and "221 (d) (3)" programs	
Rent-paying ability before supplement	Present experience	Prospective, with monthly supplement averaging $20
Total	3200	7000
Under $10	—	800
$ 10 to $ 19	100	1100
$ 20 to $ 29	1100	2000
$ 30 to $ 39	1000	1000
$ 40 to $ 49	600	600
$ 50 to $ 59	400	500
$ 60 to $ 69	—	500
$ 70 to $ 79	—	200
$ 80 to $119	—	200
$120 or more	—	—

Source: Estimates taken from testimony by Paul L. Niebanck before the Senate Subcommittee on Housing for the Elderly, *Congressional Record*, 90th Congress, 1st Session, Vol. 113, No. 113, 1967, p. 10023.

the many conditions that threaten to take it away. Independence is not viewed simply as the freedom to come and go as one likes, however, but as the security within which one can do as much or as little as he is able. Specific aids are often sought in maintaining the dwelling, preparing meals, and resolving crises.

2. *Residential concentration.* Associated with the need to support oneself and continue to be involved, residential concentration of elderly persons appears to be useful. Elderly persons interact more frequently and meaningfully with their age peers than with younger persons, where contrasts are more evident and sympathetic understanding less possible.

3. *"Hominess."* As a basic image, the elderly seem to seek a physical environment that bears some resemblance to what they have known, smaller in size and modified by a degree of peace and security not sought in earlier life. This does not preclude a change in the character of the structure, however. Many elderly persons have quickly learned to enjoy high-rise apartment living, for instance.

4. *Proximity to facilities.* Reduced mobility makes routine duties more difficult and requires that all important facilities be close at hand. Convenient stores, transit stops, and religious facilities are, for various reasons, apparently the most important to the elderly. Frequently used stores should be within a block or two. Transit stops should be on site, since they are so essential to the mobility of most elderly persons. Health centers, religious, and other facilities should be available but need not be as close.

Considering the fact that relocation is more intimately associated with housing policy than with programs of income maintenance or other social welfare matters, it would seem imperative that these criteria, as well as those concerning cost, should take primacy in planning for the needs of the relocation population. Particularly is this important in the case of the elderly, for whom the home often has such great personal meaning and who are among the most vulnerable even to minor shocks, to say nothing of major upheavals.

SOCIAL AND PSYCHOLOGICAL NEEDS

One of the most crucial ills besetting the urban elderly is that of social isolation. The unmet need for companionship often transcends the more material income and housing deprivations. This is most prevalent in renewal areas where typically about half of the elderly live alone. A feeling for the depth of their deprivation can be gained from some of the comments made by elderly men and women who were relocated from the renewal area studied in Providence:

"The main thing that elderly people need is kindness and someone to visit them because they are so lonely."

"Today, the people have no respect, sympathy, compassion or friendliness toward the old people that is needed. Isolation of the elderly is worse than cancer."

"An elderly person living alone should be visited once a week to see if he is alive or dead."

"No one comes. I am so cheered up by your visits."

"I can't get out; come talk to me—it's better than a thousand dollars in my hand."

Compounding the pains of social isolation facing so many urban elderly are the typical role changes brought about by old age. These changes, which may occur abruptly and are often interdependent, include such things as completion of the parental role; withdrawal from active community and organizational leadership; termination of marriage through death of the spouse; loss of an independent household; loss of interest in distant goals and plans; greater dependence on other individuals or society; a subordinate position to adult offspring or to social workers; and membership in groups made up largely of old people. Even for the socially integrated person, such developments present difficult adjustments.

Retirement, which for many sectors of the population seems to come at a younger and younger age, restricts, as has been noted, one's activity by limiting the money available to do things. But perhaps even more important is that it calls upon one to change one's entire social orientation, from the place of work to the home or some other focal point.[14] Depending on such factors as the degree to which nonwork interests were cultivated during the working years, such a change can either be easily accomplished or be very difficult indeed. Furthermore, the substitute roles that are developed are frequently likely to carry with them a psychological importance far beyond that which they would have had in earlier years. The opportunity to maintain a satisfying relationship to one's world, be it narrowly or broadly defined, must be retained or enhanced if relocation is to be at all successful.

As with the loss of work, a decline in physical health is laden with social and psychological overtones. Chronic illness is a frequent part of the aging process as we have known it[15], but it is the

---

14. Numerous studies have been made to discover how retired persons, women as well as men, adjust to the increased amount of leisure time available to them. See, for example: Glenn H. Beyer and Margaret E. Woods, *Living and Activity Patterns of the Aged,* Research Report No. 6 (Ithaca: Cornell University Center for Housing and Environmental Studies, 1963); Aaron Lipman, "Role Conceptions of Couples in Retirement," in *Social and Psychological Aspects of Aging,* C. Tibbitts and W. Donahue, Eds. (New York: Columbia University Press, 1962); and Bernard Kutner *et al., Five Hundred Over Sixty* (New York: Russell Sage Foundation, 1956).

15. The proportion of persons free from any chronic conditions was found to fall from about 45 percent during the middle years to about 20 percent among persons of retirement age. See Public Health Service, Division of Public Health Methods, *Health Statistics from the National Health Survey: Older Persons, Selected Health Characteristics United States* July 1957-June 1959 (Washington, D.C.: U.S. Department of Health, Education and Welfare, 1960), Table 6, p. 15.

responses to such illnesses that are sometimes more troublesome than the maladies themselves. Our society has yet to assure all of its older members that they should not fear the economic threat of illness. Nor has it completely assured them, even with the Medicare program, that they will be assisted in maintaining an independent status if they become partially restricted by their affliction or unable to pay the medical bill. Until such assurance is given, the fear of crisis will continue to weigh heavily on the attitudes of our urban elderly, who, whether or not they experience serious health problems in significantly greater proportions than do their wealthy peers, have much the greater difficulty in coping with such problems when they do arise and therefore are much more subject to involuntary institutionalization, lack of medical attention, and loss of self-respect.

Widowhood, perhaps more than any other crisis, forces the affected person into a new and disturbing relationship to the world. Women, because of the differences in age of marriage and life expectancy, are much more frequently bereft of their spouse than men, and many spend a substantial proportion of their lives in widowhood. Besides the trauma of personal loss, widowhood often carries with it a sharp reduction in income and in status, the gradual severance of important relationships, and a growing inappropriateness of the existing life style. The housing and other needs of the widow, which may be quite different from those of the married couple, should be taken seriously in any relocation or rehousing effort.

Community Services for the Elderly

It is often assumed that the elderly are somewhat insulated from the vicissitudes of life by the intensity of their religious faith. It is also presumed by many that the assistance given in various forms by children and other relatives tends to cushion the shocks and losses attendant upon old age. Neither of these hopeful claims is as true as one might wish, however. Religious attitudes, for example, are conditioned largely by one's experiences early in life, thus militating against a resurgence of interest during one's declining years.[16] As for family loyalties, it is quite clear that the multigen-

16. Paul B. Maves, "Aging Religion and the Church," in *Handbook of Social Gerontology,* C. Tibbitts, Ed. (Chicago: University of Chicago Press, 1960), pp. 698-752.

eration household is now more a historic relic than a present-day fact, and neither the younger party nor the older seems desirous of reversing the trend.

These sources of psychological and material support, while not wholly lacking, cannot usually be counted upon to relieve the burdens of old age. Thus it is that certain community services are necessary to enable the older person, particularly one who has been beset by difficulties through the years, to draw upon his own inner resources to deal adequately with life. Such services as personal counseling, senior centers and clubs, health facilities, and the like are quite common in urban areas, but even these have not begun to reach the elderly who are in greatest need.

One of the reasons for this lack of success is simply that the older person often has great difficulty expressing his more intimate or intangible needs, such as attention, status, self-confidence, and usefulness. This inability to specify needs and admit dependency makes it difficult for many services to meet any but the most outwardly apparent and pressing problems. Exacerbating the situation is the fact that relatively few community agencies are equipped to deal effectively with social and emotional needs, while extensive (though still inadequate) programs exist to deal with income and housing problems. A fundamental difficulty in delivering the service that is required stems from the general lack of trained social service personnel in the field of aging. Not only are there entirely too few social workers who have graduate professional degrees, but the tendency of even the best of them is to avoid work with older people, which seems both more difficult and inherently less productive of long-term benefits than aid to younger people. The efforts of those that do undertake such work are often restricted to medical and mental health needs, rather than to work that is concerned with the variety of problems faced by the more "normal" elderly population as a whole.[17]

A third inhibition to successful service is that each type of service agency has definite limits to its own involvement. Most senior centers, for example, serve only those elderly persons who take the initiative to come in, and therefore leave out many who are in great need of group activity and personal counseling. An-

17. See, for example, Council on Social Work Education, "Bi-Monthly News," February, 1962, p. 26.

other example is the Old Age Assistance program, in which personal contacts with elderly clients are all too often limited to the establishment of eligibility, and therefore miss an opportunity for more intensive help. Similarly, golden age clubs often have little attraction for many older persons, since their services are restricted to those that have meaning only for middle-class persons who are accustomed to club activity.

While some steps forward have been recorded in recent years, there remains a huge task in discovering satisfying roles for the elderly members of our society, promoting an acceptance of growing old on the part of that society, and assuring the elderly sector of a share in the good life. It is the latter need that remains most pressing. Only in the area of medical services has there been significant advance in the equalization of distribution of goods and services, and even here our country is admittedly far behind most of the other advanced nations. All too many elderly persons needlessly live out the balance of their lives in institutions, and for all too many others only a semblance of independence is retained and the word "choice" has little, if any, meaning.

Effects of Relocation

This chapter has depicted the general situation in which our urban elderly population finds itself, and has suggested that the elderly in renewal areas and other older areas are even more vulnerable to shock and additional deprivations than the elderly population as a whole. An elderly couple dislodged by urban renewal is, for example, about twice as likely to have an income under $2000 as its counterpart living in an area unaffected by renewal. Similarly, an elderly individual living alone in a renewal area is 50 percent more likely to have an income under $1000 than one living outside a renewal area.

In housing, the same pattern prevails. Housing occupied by the elderly is in general old; in renewal areas it is older. In general it is in moderately poor condition; in renewal areas it is much worse. Housing values are generally low; in renewal areas they are lower. Though ownership is still common for elderly renewal area residents, the prevalence of low-income and single-person households tends to undermine even this outwardly favorable characteristic.

Similarly, older persons in renewal areas are likely either to be suffering from health disabilities more than their peers elsewhere, or are less able to cope with these disabilities. The same generalization applies to social and psychological problems, which if not more common are borne less easily in deprived areas and are dealt with less effectively by the institutions designed to serve them. While personal suffering is difficult to measure directly, all the indirect indices disclose that the elderly relocatee is, by and large, very likely to suffer from multiple deprivations more than almost any other sector of the urban population.

Involuntary displacement can often accentuate or intensify these problems. The impact of relocation on income and housing has already been noted. It has been found that the impact on such things as social ties, behavior patterns, mental health, and personal expectations in some cases can be devastating. The more advanced the age, the greater the difficulty in making rapid adaptations, and while negative responses to relocation are hardly universal, it is not unheard of for the response of an older person to take the form of extreme withdrawal or even premature death. The implications of these findings have obvious importance for relocation policy, and will be addressed throughout the remainder of this report. While attention in the next chapter will remain focused on the elderly, it will be broadened in Chapter 5 to include the younger members of the relocation population as well. This is appropriate in view of the fact that the experiences faced by the elderly, while often comparatively more severe, are nevertheless typical of those faced by their younger counterparts, and the younger sectors are not necessarily any better able to deal with them when they arise.

4

KNOWLEDGE GAINED THROUGH THE DEMONSTRATION STUDIES[1]

Clearly, involuntary relocation creates special difficulties for the elderly person. It is also clear that the relocation agency often is hard put to deal with these problems. The demonstration projects associated with this study were undertaken in order to understand better the nature of the burden that the elderly bear and to discover what realistic steps might be taken to improve the agency's capacity for service.

The four projects were in no way designed as strict research experiments, with rigid testing of hypotheses. Rather, they were set up as exploratory investigations in a variety of settings, with a variety of clients, served by a variety of agencies. In a real sense, they are representative of situations involving large numbers of displaced households. On the other hand, the selection was hardly random, since the timing of the study had to be matched at least in part by the timing of the particular redevelopment project, and the cities chosen had to contain agencies that were sufficiently skilled to develop and administer an ameliorative program and an

---

1. These studies are reported more fully in four separate reports, all of which are available from the Institute for Environmental Studies, University of Pennsylvania: *Relocation of the Dispossessed Elderly: A Study of Mexican-Americans,* by Julie M Reich, Michael A. Stegman and Nancy W. Stegman (1966). A report on the San Antonio project. *Preparing the Elderly for Relocation: A Study of Isolated Persons,* by Wallace F. Smith (1966). A report on the San Francisco demonstration project. *The Social Functioning of the Dislodged Elderly: A Study of Post-Relocation Assistance,* by David Joyce, Robert R. Mayer, and Mary K. Nenno (1966). A report on the Providence project. *Advocacy and Service for the Elderly Relocatee,* by Juliet F. Brudney (1968). A report on the New York City project.

individual or organization able to provide professional advice on the research aspects, to evaluate the results, and to prepare materials for the final report.

With these criteria in mind, San Antonio, San Francisco, New York, and Providence were selected as the locations of the demonstration projects. In San Antonio, the sponsoring organization was an arm of the Community Welfare Council. In San Francisco, it was the social action section of the Council of Churches. In New York, it was a confederation of settlement houses. In Providence, it was the official relocation agency. Each project is described below, in turn, and the individual descriptions are followed by a discussion of problems and conclusions common to several or all the demonstrations.

SAN ANTONIO: RELOCATING THE DISPOSSESSED ELDERLY

The San Antonio project was sponsored by the San Antonio Community Welfare Council and directed by Senior Community Services, Inc., a community agency devoted entirely to the welfare of the elderly. It was designed to focus attention on a group of elderly persons who, at the time the demonstration began, were faced with imminent displacement from the Rosa Verde renewal area, a Spanish-speaking, Mexican-American community located on the periphery of the downtown business district. Though most of its residents had lived in the United States for many years, they had retained many of their Mexican customs, which provided greater support for older persons than customs in the "Anglo" community normally do. Extended family ties, courtyard living arrangements, and active religious life were manifestations of the supportive environment. The residents regarded renewal activities as a threat to their way of life, particularly since previous relocation efforts in a similar neighborhood had failed to give adequate attention to the inhabitants' special cultural desires.

The project proposed to study ways of bringing the special relocation needs engendered both by cultural differences and advanced age to the attention of the relocation and welfare agencies of the community. Particularly, it was hoped that a means would be found to train Old Age Assistance workers to enhance their ability to perform casework, and to use their skills in helping elderly persons meet the demands of relocation, whether or not they were receiving financial aid from the OAA program. In the course of the demonstration, it was hoped that insights could be gained in working with the older Mexican-American that would lead to better service for members of other ethnic minority groups elsewhere, who, through the interaction of discrimination and poverty, live in central city slums and, by that fact, bear a disproportionate part of the burden of relocation.

The changeable nature of renewal and other governmental plans has been one of the difficulties confronting those who administer relocation programs. It might thus be considered appropriate that the demonstration projects had to adjust to this uncertainty. Indeed, the San Antonio demonstration faced two such problems. The first arose when the State Old Age Assistance office found it impossible, for internal reasons, to participate in the program. The second arose when the local renewal agency decided to delay the Rosa Verde renewal project in favor of a more pressing need for clearance in the area designated for the impending "Hemisfair," an area containing comparatively few elderly residents.

By the time it became apparent that the demonstration would involve only token relocation during the life of the research project, the investigation of the relocation process in San Antonio and of the client population in Rosa Verde had proceeded far enough to show strongly that more adequate plans were needed than were customarily made prior to actually engaging in the movement of people. There was particular need for development of new essential community resources and for better coordination of those already existing. The demonstration project retained its *raison d'etre,* therefore, by concentrating its attention on the prerelocation period and attempting to identify the kind of planning that is necessary before relocation actually takes place.

To understand better the needs and desires of the potential elderly relocatees, the study reviewed the relevant census materials and information already collected by the renewal agency, and undertook to interview the elderly themselves. The survey revealed clearly their extreme poverty and the inability of many to obtain even minimal welfare payments; the impossibility, therefore, of asking them to pay higher rents even for improved living conditions; the mediocre state of their health, which contributed an additional handicap; and the inability of many to cope with

English or even official Spanish, so that they failed to understand the relocation information they had received in formal communications.

Two major problems presented themselves in developing a plan for relocation. The first revolved around the great gap between the long-standing needs of the residents and the services available to meet these needs. Such a gap exists to a greater or lesser degree throughout the country, but in San Antonio the deficiencies in welfare payments and other services were particularly great, especially for noncitizens. About this, the project could do little beyond exploring its extent and strongly recommending a greater commitment of funds for welfare services and a relaxation in eligibility requirements. Since the project's termination in the spring of 1965, some of the recommendations have been adopted.

The second problem proved more amenable to immediate solution. At the start of the project, there seemed to be a strong degree of rigid separation and even distrust among existing agencies. Furthermore, a communications barrier existed not only between agency and agency but between agencies and their clients. Confronted with a shortage of workers and funds, agencies gave help when approached but made little effort to reach into the community to find clients who might be in serious need but who did not know how to obtain help. Moreover, many workers or agencies had chosen to focus their attention on children or younger adults, where needs seemed more easily met and the results of aid of longer duration. Concomitantly, there was a tendency for them to look askance at the renewal agency, fearing that its activities might add to their already overburdened caseloads.

To relieve some of the rigidity in the social welfare system, and to promote coordination of activities and a better understanding of the human needs in renewal, the project organized a six-week training course for workers from various public and private community agencies. Half the discussions were led by agency representatives, to acquaint personnel with each other's work, and half by representatives from the Worden School of Social Work, to familiarize all personnel with casework practice. The program was successful not only in the skills and knowledge imparted to individual workers but also in promoting interagency harmony. Each participant became familiar with the goals and problems of each agency, and the understanding and empathy that resulted are believed to have made significant differences in the manner in which subsequent cases have been handled.

The major gain of the project was this demonstration of the ability to develop greater cooperation among community agencies and more sensitivity to the special problems of elderly relocatees, particularly those in an ethnic environment. This change has been evidenced in a number of recognizable ways since the project's termination. Indeed, it can be claimed that the project was not merely a temporary manifestation of concern, but a continuing force in the progress of social services in the city of San Antonio.

To further these gains, the demonstration suggests a number of changes in policy, which are included in Chapter 5 of this volume. Among the more important is the appeal that in future renewal projects the period between the socioeconomic survey and property acquisition be used productively to develop contacts and establish rapport with the elderly. Results of the survey should be distributed to all community agencies, so they can better mobilize and adapt their programs to meet the demands which relocation will make upon them. Social and health service agencies should cooperate in establishing a committee to plan the improvement of gerontological services. One recommendation for a specific change in relocation practice has emerged: that consideration should be given to group relocation of members of ethnic minorities who prefer to remain living closely together.

San Francisco: Preparing the Elderly for Relocation

Although relocation may foster or reveal difficulties which require the services of a trained social worker or other professional for solution, there are certain other services which can be rendered by any physically capable sympathetic person. Sponsored by the San Francisco Council of Churches, and conducted by its Social Service Department, which already had experience with volunteers, the project in San Francisco was designed to determine to what degree volunteers could be used to improve the relocation services already offered by the San Francisco Redevelopment Agency. The volunteers were to be recruited from churches in the project area, the Western Addition renewal area, and hence were to be persons directly familiar with the neighborhood and the problems its residents faced, but trained and directed by experienced social workers to make best use of their knowledge and concern. Individual relocatees were to be reached through a friendly visiting program and through nonsectarian senior centers located in the local churches.

Like the San Antonio project, that in San Francisco had to be adjusted to meet a change in the renewal program. The demonstration project began while the renewal program for the area was still in the planning stage. This would have permitted work with the elderly persons to begin as soon as the relocatees were identified by the redevelopment agency, and to continue through the relocation process, when it would have supplemented the efforts of the public relocation workers. Just before formal approval of the redevelopment project by the Urban Renewal Administration, however, an initiative amendment to the California constitution was adopted which had the effect of preventing the redevelopment agency from requiring that private rehabilitators or builders meet the fair housing requirements of the federal renewal program. Consequently, the URA declared all California agencies ineligible for redevelopment grants for projects involving private residential renewal. The amendment was challenged in the courts, but plans for Western Addition faced indefinite delay.[2]

Adapting itself to this development, the project's objective became that of preparing individuals so that they could cope with relocation as a normal problem of living, rather than a traumatic experience. By improving the overall functioning of the disadvantaged elderly, removing sources of disabilities, strengthening their self-confidence, and providing social supports, it was posited that they would become capable of adjusting to displacement when it occurred. Although the 112 elderly households and individuals who formed the caseload in San Francisco on the average had higher incomes than those encountered in many similar areas, interviews revealed that they were still beset with many pressing needs. The familiar ills of isolation, poor health, and substandard housing were all prevalent, and poverty was by no means absent.

The project used volunteers in the two ways that had been initially envisioned. Although it had been expected that the client

2. In fact, it was not until June, 1967, that the adjudication was finally settled, with a U.S. Supreme Court ruling that the amendment was contrary to the federal Constitution.

population would be divided among the two operating programs, it was found in practice that on occasion the same clients participated in both. Friendly visiting acted as a preparatory program for participation in the senior center activities. It also had importance of its own, however, since some clients had problems which could be better served through an individual rather than a group contact, and many clients had no inclination or ability to participate in the more active program. The individual volunteer, meanwhile, worked exclusively in either one program or the other, and was given intensive training in either individual or group work before undertaking any project activities.

At the centers, the relatively gregarious elderly participated in recreational activities, discussion groups, and in the learning of crafts, such as weaving and ceramics. These programs were conducted on a social group rather than an individual basis, with the view not simply of providing recreation but of strengthening individuals through satisfying social experiences. The visiting service, on the other hand, concentrated on the more withdrawn or physically incapacitated older persons and depended upon a relationship of personal trust. Volunteer visitors, each of whom was responsible to only a small group of clients, not only gave direct aid themselves but helped identify those requiring referral to other appropriate community services.

The community service network was found to be reasonably adequate in the financial and medical help it was able to give, but nearly devoid of any counseling services which often, for the elderly, are as urgent as more material aid. The greatest material lack, which would have proved more serious if relocation had in fact been carried out, was an inadequate allowance for rent in public welfare grants. The project found some tendency for elderly persons to use poor housing as a means of self-punishment or as an expression of a sense of personal unworthiness. Nevertheless, those without such psychological difficulties also lived in poor housing, and there seems to have been a serious shortage of low-rent, standard quality, private housing, and the amount of public housing was altogether insufficient to make up for the deficiency in the private sector.

To gain some exposure to the problems directly related to relocation, the project brought within its caseload a few elderly persons facing displacement because of code enforcement and public works projects. This limited experience served to support the belief that prerelocation psychological and material support would facilitate adaptation to rehousing. One area of particular hardship was uncovered, however, the rectification of which would require an explicit change in the procedures of the relocation agency. Groups of interdependent neighbors were found, whose members are often as close as those of the same household, but who are never treated as such in relocation. For such individuals, group relocation is suggested. The best means toward this end may lie in finding a private philanthropy associated with the group through ethnic or other ties, which would be willing to finance and operate a residence building for their use, although public housing might be used where it is in sufficient supply.

In sum, the project functioned as an intermediary in the welfare process, providing psychological support and other services itself, but referring those in greater need to the appropriate agencies and helping them in claiming and receiving aid. Volunteers proved to be capable and reliable in both the friendly visiting and the senior center programs, when properly trained and supervised. The desirability of continuing a similar program on a permanent city-wide basis was recommended on the basis of the project experience.

NEW YORK: ADVOCACY AND SERVICE FOR THE ELDERLY RELOCATEE

The New York demonstration was concerned with the entire relocation process. It began by selecting 148 elderly households at random in the West Side urban renewal area, determining their needs prior to relocation, aiding them in selecting and moving to a new residence and in adjusting to their postrelocation situation. The renewal plan for this area, a twenty-block neighborhood in Manhattan, centered around a comprehensive design which involved the conservation of many buildings and staged redevelopment, including construction of a public housing project with some specially designed apartments for the elderly on which eligible relocatees had priority. Occupants of houses in the area of the first stage were to be quartered temporarily in buildings in later stages, acquired and operated by the city. They were then to return either to rehabilitated or new units in their previous neighborhood. Though this "on-siting" involved two moves instead of one, it was believed that giving households the opportunity to return permanently to their original neighborhood would be worth this inconvenience. The renewal plans for the area were carried out with only normal delays, and the large public housing project was completed within the life of the demonstration. Hence, "Project Janus," as the demonstration was called, was able to carry through its work largely as originally planned.

Project Janus was sponsored by the United Neighborhood Houses of New York City. It had two general goals. First, it wished to develop a comprehensive diagnostic interview that would identify needs for service and anticipate the degree of difficulty that would be occasioned by relocation in individual cases. Second, it wished to determine from what sources volunteers could be recruited and how valuable their services would be, under professional supervision, in aiding elderly persons meet the problems inherent in dislocation.

The diagnostic interview schedule that was developed covered general demographic information; the respondent's knowledge of his need for moving and how he had acquired the knowledge; his housing desires, including his knowledge of, and desire for, on-siting and final rehousing in the renewed neighborhood; his plans for obtaining an apartment, including his knowledge of relocation benefits; his present living arrangements, ownership of furniture and household goods; his housing expenses and his financial capability for adequately housing himself; his family situation; his health; and his shopping habits and other uses of the neighborhood.

The interviewer, in obtaining this comprehensive knowledge, was by no means a neutral poll-taker. Rather, the opening interview was used as a means of establishing rapport and of replacing any misinformation the client might have with correct information concerning his rights to aid, his opportunities, and his responsibilities. A tentative "relocation plan" for each client was developed, based on information drawn from the interview, and the results were supplied to the city relocation worker.

The lengthy interview was found to be unnecessarily unwieldy. Much of the general material, concerning such things as education and citizenship, which was expected to provide the basis for preliminary overall estimates of need, proved to have no relevance to the actual services requested or provided. Analysis of the statistical materials showed no way to differentiate between those who were more heavily and less heavily served in the course of the project. Those within these categories were distinguished, not according to the crude indicators possible to include in a questionnaire, but rather by subtle differences in personality or in family relationships, or even by the relative ability and devotion of individual relocation workers or welfare workers of whose caseloads they formed a part. A shortened interview, used as a means of introduction and to formulate tentative relocation plans, subject to probable revision as the client became better known, would be equally valuable and considerably easier to administer.

In the development of the volunteer corps, which ultimately carried the major responsibility for service, the project found both interest and capability. Volunteers came primarily from two sources: people living in the neighborhood, who became acquainted with Janus' work through its local office and activities; and teenagers, recruited through school programs. Other, more specialized sources, were also tapped to a limited extent. Peace Corps trainees proved particularly helpful, being enthusiastic, energetic, and warmly accepted by the relocatees themselves.

Whether considering the activities of the professional staff or the volunteers, the project acted largely in the role of an unofficial ombudsman. It uncovered major deficiencies in the amounts of aid being received by persons who were fully eligible for and in need of such aid. These gaps existed both in the immediate relocation program with which the project was primarily concerned and in city welfare programs generally. The deficiencies stemmed from many factors: inadequate regulations; poor administrative procedures; unnecessarily rigid policies originating at the top of the official hierarchy; poor communication between office personnel and field workers; and indifferent or incompetent people in either the office or the field. It is impossible, of course, to measure the relative extent of these deficiencies against the great assistance rendered by official agencies, and unnecessary in fact to do so. Even though only a very small minority of individuals who are entitled by law to certain benefits may not receive them, whether because of official acts of omission or commission, there is a proper function for a trained intermediary to assist them, and it is this role that was performed by the Janus staff. Its importance is revealed not only in the story of the relief afforded to those officially its clients, but also in the services it found impossible to deny to others in the neighborhood, who were attracted by its store-front office or learned from grateful clients of the assistance rendered them. The Janus project, like that of San Francisco, thus raises the question of the need for some service outside of the official complex of welfare and relocation activities, to inform, protect, and make demands in behalf of relocatees incapable of performing these functions for themselves.

PROVIDENCE: THE SOCIAL FUNCTIONING OF THE DISLODGED ELDERLY

Prior study of difficulties faced by elderly relocatees had suggested that one of the greatest areas of need, if not indeed the greatest, lay in an inability to renew or make new contacts with social agencies and to find a comfortable niche of friendships and informal services in the social structure of the new neighborhood. The demonstration in Providence was planned to investigate the impact of the forced movement on the social functioning of individuals who had been relocated, and to develop services which could be offered by the relocation service to counteract any ill effects after rehousing was accomplished. Unlike the other demonstrations, it was conducted by a public agency, the Family and Business Relocation Service (FRS), a centralized relocation bureau established by the city in 1949. Several months before undertaking this project, the FRS had completed relocation of families from the Central Classical renewal area. Although a physically substandard rooming house district, this area was well serviced by neighborhood facilities, and was situated in close proximity to the central business district of Providence. Many elderly persons lived in the area, and the FRS had been sufficiently concerned about their special needs to employ a staff person to provide relocation aid solely to older persons. Once rehoused, however, the relocatees had not been assisted further prior to the initiation of the demonstration.

In order to determine what aid was necessary, the FRS contracted with the Rhode Island Council of Community Services (CCS) to interview all individuals and households relocated from the Central Classical area who could be identified as over 62 years of age, to determine their demographic characteristics, and the differences between their housing, income, health, and social functioning before and after their move.

After the initial interviews, the FRS conducted a ten-month service program, in which a professional caseworker offered service appropriate to each individual's needs. Although the initial interview by the CCS was used to determine the order in which visits should be made, the social worker revisited each relocatee to determine the precise nature of the problem and the aid which could be offered. Friendly visiting, counseling, transportation aid, and most importantly, referral to existing social agencies were all part of the program.

The CCS conducted a second set of interviews a year and a half after relocation to measure the long-term effect of relocation and the particular benefits derived from the service program. The first interview had shown that poor social functioning was widespread, and had worsened in the course of and following dislocation. Widows experienced the gravest discomforts, but as many as two-thirds of all the households needed some assistance in adapting to their new environment. Housing situations, on the whole, were generally improved. Sixty percent of the relocatees were found to be more satisfied with their new housing, in contrast to only 20 percent who were less satisfied. Those who moved into Dexter Manor, a public housing development solely for the elderly, were among the most successfully relocated persons. Income was by and large unaffected by the forced move, although the cost of living often rose. The few individuals who lost their business endured the greatest financial setbacks. Neighborhood facilities were generally as satisfactory and even more convenient in the new environment, although church facilities, in particular, were typically more inconvenient, particularly since many continued to regard a church in their old neighborhood as their home church. Many, also, missed the activities of the central business district, and were unable to spare bus fare from their meager funds for even one trip a month to the center of the city.

Displacement thus caused some discomfort in regard to housing, health, income, and use of neighborhood facilities. The harmful impact was typically small, however, and affected a minority of the relocatees. In many instances, the results may have even been beneficial. The most pervasive and serious disruption was in socialization patterns. Nearly all experienced a loss of friends and social contacts, and all had to adjust to a new social environment. Some found this task exceedingly difficult.

The broad measurement device used in the second interview revealed little overall improvement in the lot of these elderly during the service period, although welfare benefits and medical care had been obtained by some as a result of the referrals made by the project caseworker. Success in dealing with the aged, however, might best be determined by the degree to which decline is arrested rather than improvement gained; and no worsening was noted in this period. Close evaluation of individual cases, moreover, illustrated that the small gestures and personal favors performed by the FRS caseworker, in addition to the referrals for major needs, often had unexpectedly large beneficial effects. Loneliness and insecurity are critical problems which can be exacerbated by relocation, but apparently eased for many by even minimal evidences of friendship and concern.

From the project study and its prior experience, FRS now recommends that relocation aid be provided from twelve to eighteen months before property acquisition until at least six months and in some cases two years after relocation. Throughout this period, the relocation agency should maintain close and constant contact with the affected persons, making maximum use of existing agencies in the delivery of service. A second major recommendation calls for the establishment of neighborhood social service centers for the elderly. In addition to bringing help within walking distance, such centers would provide informed counselors, a focal point of recreation in which to make friends, and a place in which emergency needs could be more easily handled.

Vital Issues in the Demonstration Studies

Because of the disparity of the programs undertaken, and particularly the absence of relocation in two of the projects, little light can be shed by these demonstrations on the question of whether relocation creates, worsens, or simply uncovers problems confronting the elderly who live in relocation areas. As with so many social questions, the answer would seem to be that the impact varies with the individual, and there seems little to be gained from determining the proportion in need which results from or is revealed by the process. There can be no doubt that elderly relocatees have a right to help from society, in moving, in reconstituting their social ties, and in confronting problems of living that existed prior to relocation and continue subsequent to it.

Low-Cost Housing

A need directly related to relocation, and common to all the demonstration cities, is that for adequate low-cost housing. In New York, whose housing supply is possibly the tightest in the country, much of the project time was expended in attending to deficiencies in the living units of on-sited tenants, which often lacked facilities or were in disrepair. In Providence, rentals were not the focus of the study, so that only indirect conclusions can be drawn. The fact that many of the elderly had been offered and accepted housing only at a great distance from the center of the city, while for valid social reasons they preferred to be close to it, would indicate a shortage of supply. In San Francisco, the major deficiency in the material benefits provided by the social service network was the allowance for rent. In San Antonio, incomes in general were so low that many could not meet even the minimum rental for public housing, which was in short supply, and decent private housing was far beyond their means.

Public housing, when properly conceived and constructed, can markedly ease the strains of dislocation. The interviews conducted in two of the projects, San Antonio and Providence, dealt in some depth with the elderly's attitudes toward this type of housing, since both cities had newly constructed projects exclusively for the elderly and planned to construct more. In New York, many of the on-sited tenants planned to relocate permanently in a project being constructed in the renewal area, and some already had done so before the demonstration was completed.

There is strong evidence in favor of housing projects designed exclusively for the elderly. In both cities which had such projects, they were beset with long waiting lists. These projects have many physical features designed to assist the older person, and they offer facilities for social and health services as well. They are very close to the central business district, transportation services, and important neighborhood facilities. These factors, together with the absence of noisy children and the opportunity to socialize freely with peers, largely explain the favorable reception. Projects in Providence which housed a heterogeneous population were in general disliked even by those who had voluntarily moved to them, and while the response to such housing in New York was on the whole positive, the fact remains that a great many elderly persons have strong preferences for age-segregated living arrangements.

The response to public housing was not universally enthusiastic, however. Both the Providence and San Antonio studies conclude that most of the elderly simply prefer to have their own private living quarters, in small structures and familiar surroundings. This was especially the case for the Mexican-Americans in Rosa Verde who feared a break with their secure ethnic neighborhood. Of those who expressed specific dislike for public housing, about half held misconceptions, but half based their opinion realistically on existing restrictions and facilities. The prohibition against pets, the lack of sufficient space, and too many questions about the past were some of the most frequently expressed complaints. Nevertheless, public housing emerged as a positive force in the lives of many elderly relocatees, and those who moved into these developments frequently showed dramatic improvements in their physical care and their social life. Many of the objections to public housing do not stem from its public sponsorship but from relatively minor matters that can be cured by a more sympathetic design or a change in operating policy.

Inadequacies of Community Welfare Services

Another, clearer, theme to emerge from the demonstrations is the great deficiency of community agencies, both public and private, in serving the needs of the elderly. Beset by inadequate funding and already overburdened staff, most agencies are understandably content to serve those who come to them, without looking for additional clients who may be in greater need, or even making a positive attempt to render maximum service to clients already on their rosters.

The blame for such neglect does not lie completely with lack of financial resources or skilled personnel, although these are certainly crucial. Operational imperfections of the service agencies on occasion contribute materially to their ineffectiveness. One of the most important of these imperfections is the lack of coherent, defined purposes on the part of many agencies and their personnel, and of an evaluative procedure to determine how well the purposes are being met. The experience in New York's West Side is illustrative. There the three public agencies concerned with renewal operated with intricate policies determined at the highest levels in each agency, though sometimes in conflict with each other. Communication from the central office to the field worker was not sufficient to insure the carrying out of the avowed policy, however, even when it was procedurally possible to do so. When the representatives of these agencies themselves were uncertain about correct policies and procedures, the troubled elderly had no means of obtaining the benefits to which they were entitled. Even though carried on with knowledge by skilled workers, Janus' efforts were frequently frustrated. The absence of clear-cut objectives also prevented the agencies from setting a valid basis for evaluating the success of the field operations, so that a self-corrective process could evolve.

The degree of cooperation among community agencies also leaves much to be desired. A lack of rapport among agencies was frequently evidenced in the demonstration cities. Service agencies were often unaware of one another's functions and seldom provided sufficient referral services to their respective clients. On occasion, such disorder even degenerated into interagency conflict and jealousy.

The harmonious interrelationship of agencies, together with a coherent sense of purpose in each individual agency, would substantially enhance a community service network's ability to extend itself to help the needy elderly. It would also make apparent any gaps in the net which are not filled at all by any of the agencies. Such an upgrading in service would have profound implications for relocation. With their ills treated routinely in advance, the aged should be in a better position to cope with the discomforts of dislocation when they occur. If troubles arise during or after relocation, the more responsive service agencies should be able to alleviate them quickly. In any case, whether help is administered before, during, or after relocation, a vigorous city-wide service network is invaluable in making the transition required by dislocation a smooth and positive one.

Role of the Relocation Agency

In the face of the need for improvement in the entire service complex, a question arises as to the proper role of the local relocation agency. Should its scope be limited to housing referrals, payment of moving expenses, and physical aids directly related to moving? Or should its perspective be broadened to encompass multifaceted social, health, and financial needs as well? The individual demonstration projects came to different conclusions, arising at least partly from the different positions from which they approached the question. San Francisco's recommendation is for a restricted public role, while Providence calls for an expanded role. This is not surprising, since the San Francisco demonstration concentrated on prerelocation work with individuals, strengthening them to meet relocation as only one problem among the many they must face. Such broad service is clearly beyond the scope of a relocation agency. In Providence, on the other hand, the relocation agency itself conducted the demonstration project, and having had successful prior experience with extended services to elderly persons, it not unnaturally concluded that this was among its proper duties.

As one considers the actual work undertaken by the demonstrations that is normally handled by a relocation agency, however, each of the extreme positions become untenable, and the real question becomes one of where on the continuum the relocation agency of any particular city should settle. Obviously, the rehousing assistance offered by the agency must receive top priority. Nevertheless, in dealing with people about to be displaced, relocation officials frequently come across individuals having serious and long-standing unmet needs. Their contact with these troubled persons provides an excellent opportunity to procure for them the necessary assistance. Limiting relocation aid only to needs that are visibly associated with housing seems, in these cases at least, to be out of order from a human standpoint, and such a narrow perspective may even interfere with the efficiency of relocation itself. San Francisco and New York both found that patient counseling and administration of other services were essential before some elderly persons could make sound decisions about where they should relocate. San Antonio similarly found a pressing need for greater attention to individual concerns before movement could be undertaken. Likewise, the need for services does not stop once a move has been made. Indeed, it was found, in Providence, that the long-range social impact of relocation could be quite harmful even in cases where the change in housing was generally beneficial.

Whether the agency itself should undertake to meet these uncovered or created needs would seem to be not so much a matter of theory as of the circumstances of the individual city. In a city where there is already a social service network capable of meeting the needs imposed or exposed by dislocation, the relocation agency may well restrict itself to referring those it finds in need to the proper established agencies, with its workers otherwise limiting themselves to rehousing aid. In other places, the agency may find that it must itself deal with the problems it uncovers. Local relocation agencies, that is, must view the entire relocation process in a broad frame of reference. Accordingly, they should conduct frequent home visits in which they inform clients of their rights, provide them with the available material aid, counsel them when needed, and, quite importantly, insure that those revealing unserved needs—of any kind—are referred to the appropriate resources of the community, either within the agency itself or in other agencies. As relocation agencies move in this direction, with the widespread institutionalization of such elements as visiting services, senior citizen centers, interagency training programs, and neighborhood social service centers, relocation will reach the stage where it is a positive force in the lives of those it affects.

Institutionalizing Needed Services

A related, though not identical, question is that of whether the kinds of functions that were performed by the demonstration projects should be the on-going concern of public or private agencies. Each of the demonstrations operated to some degree as middlemen in the welfare process, providing links between needy elderly persons and appropriate services, scrutinizing and spurring the performance of community agencies. Opinion varies as to whether this intermediary role can be more effective when performed by an existing governmental unit, possibly in the relocation agency itself, or by an independent group prodding from the outside.

The decision partially depends upon the precise program desired. The concept of neighborhood social service centers for the elderly, advocated by the Providence project, is geared toward making the existing public and private agencies alike more accessible and increasing their ability to serve the aged. The accessibility of valuable services, in both a physical and psychic sense, would be enhanced, and sensitivity to local needs on the part of the participating agencies would be increased. The establishment of such centers could readily be incorporated in the functioning of existing city agencies.

Similarly, the approach used in San Antonio might best be handled by governmental agencies. The interagency training course prompted agencies to define their objectives and promoted interagency contacts. Agency personnel attending such a course became more alert to the services offered, and more explicitly conscious of their own particular tasks. Once begun, there would seem to be no reason why city agencies could not continue such a program.

The New York project, on the other hand, saw a clear need to instigate improvement of the service network from without. The size of New York's governmental machinery may intensify the difficulties of having policies reviewed or complaints handled through official channels, particularly among agencies with equal status but different goals. Whatever the reason, the project advocated greater citizen participation in the form of review boards for all public service agencies and a tenant-directed housing service in each renewal district. Such citizen committees were viewed as the only effective means of securing proper service from existing agencies.

San Francisco took a neutral position on this question. Friendly visiting and church-based senior citizen centers were emphasized, and services like these are a "natural" for private organizations. Yet without a large-scale public commitment, these programs are not inclusive enough to improve the overall condition of the elderly in older urban areas. The project indeed acknowledged that the primary responsibility rests with public agencies, which must themselves devise a more effective and responsible service network.

What, then, is the best course to follow in institutionalizing the valuable functions performed by the service projects? Friendly visiting, church centers, interagency training programs, and neighborhood service centers provide a harmonious set of tools which appear to be generally of assistance. Local differences will condition precisely which of these should be under private and public auspices. But, whatever the mixture that evolves, it may become necessary, where bureaucratic inefficiencies inhibit the granting and obtaining of benefits by individual clients, to encourage active citizen committees or some other appropriate watchdog mechanism.

Centralized Relocation Services

The obvious needs for efficient operation, equal treatment, comprehensive services, and positive relocation demand that the relocation function be centralized, in the manner of Providence's FRS. With the responsibility for all relocation fixed upon a central agency, the very concept of relocation gains in stature, and is thereby more likely to command the cooperation of other agencies

There is also a need for administrative centralization within service agencies. New York's experience showed that an excessive dispersion of authority discouraged the responsible administration of relocation activities. The New York City Department of Relocation gave the job of providing relocation services for West Side residents to a special management corporation created by the Department of Real Estate. Plagued by poor lines of communication and unclear directives, the corporation was highly deficient in servicing its clients. In San Antonio, similar disarray was noted.

In essence, then, many service organizations appear to be suffering from poor internal administration. Many of them are structured all too loosely and haphazardly. While decentralization of activities can be effective, it must be carried out with firm direction from the top. For example, an on-site relocation office or a neighborhood service center can greatly facilitate the delivery of services, but the field office must be provided with clear goals and responsible policy guidelines.

Importance of the Prerelocation Period

The demonstration projects all emphasized the crucial importance of the prerelocation period in effecting successful relocation. The experiences of on-siting in New York illustrated most dramatically the dangers inherent in this period. With permanent relocation imminent, there was little incentive to improve temporary housing conditions. Among other disturbing consequences, structures deteriorated, vagrancy mushroomed, and vandalism increased. Many of the tenants responded by leaving the area early and completely foregoing their relocation rights. In San Francisco, the delay in renewal led to similarly poor housing situations and, most notably, to a rise in rents. In some instances, it was found that private landlords, fearful of losing rents, deliberately failed to distribute eviction notices to tenants. Motivated by uncertainty, suspicion, and anger, many San Franciscans also moved hastily from suddenly unbearable surroundings. It is clear, then, that the strains induced in the prerelocation period can be even more oppressive than those caused by actual dislocation itself.

There will inevitably be a time lag between a project's initiation and its implementation. San Francisco and San Antonio both demonstrated the wisdom of preplanning during this period. The resources of the relocation service should be set in motion to determine the specific needs of those to be affected and to plan appropriate courses of action. The expeditious implementation of renewal in a straightforward and honest manner is desirable from all standpoints.

Some doubt has been raised about using the interview results obtained during the planning period for overall area plans. Elderly relocatees, in particular, seem to suffer from a lapse of memory or a desire to please the interviewer, which sometimes renders the information collected of dubious reliability. Irrespective of their precision for overall planning purposes, however, these interviews are invaluable as instruments for discovering and serving individual needs.

Training and Use of Volunteers

Among the most important conclusions that can be drawn from the demonstrations is that volunteers can be very useful in strengthening the relocation effort. In both the New York and San Francisco projects, extensive reliance was placed on their work, and success was obvious. Although Providence had not planned to make use of volunteer services, a volunteer friendly visiting program emerged, which has since been formally organized throughout Rhode Island. It was the finding of both the San Francisco and Providence studies that the foremost ill confronting aged persons is loneliness or emotional isolation. Both studies provided considerable evidence that, even in cities where material welfare benefits approach adequacy, the unmet need for companionship often remains, and that volunteers can be quite useful in the satisfaction of this need.

The demonstration experiences offer four useful guidelines for the successful utilization of volunteer help by community agencies. First, they should receive extended in-service training, bulwarked by the use of practical materials from field experience. This training should be well planned, and should proceed in a structured and rather formal manner. Second, it is advisable, if possible, to have volunteers work in or near an area in which they reside. Their familiarity with the particular locality increases their usefulness to clients. Third, it is essential to insure guidance and review of volunteer efforts, so that clients in need of professional help obtain it immediately and so that the motivation and ability of the volunteers are sustained. Fourth, volunteers should be relied upon largely for only practical assistance and for supportive friendly attentions. Complex cases and counseling should remain the prerogative of specialized workers.

SUMMARY

The demonstration projects differed considerably in the approaches they took and in their connection with the relocation process. Yet, they have much in common.

The San Antonio project was concerned with the need for careful planning of relocation, particularly for the elderly members of an ethnic minority. A survey of the characteristics, needs, and desires of the elderly Mexican-Americans in the redevelopment area served as a basis for developing more appropriate and realistic rehousing plans for them. A major block to a successful program, however, lay in the lack of understanding and communication among diverse social welfare agencies. To promote understanding of and commitment to the needs of the elderly and of the goals and working methods of each agency, the project organized and conducted a successful in-service training program.

The San Francisco project was also concerned with creating a more responsive social service network, but concentrated its efforts on testing the usefulness of a volunteer program. In its program of service to the elderly, it used a two-pronged approach, with church centers for group work activities and friendly visiting for more personal assistance. Stressing the period before relocation, the project's activities grew out of the notion that the integration of an individual in the society around him substantially enhances his ability to adjust to a forced move.

The New York demonstration carried a body of randomly selected clients through the entire relocation process. Its primary purposes were to develop and test a diagnostic interview schedule and to determine the usefulness of volunteers in the relocation process. It found the interview useful as a means of meeting potential clients and for preliminary efforts at making individual relocation plans, but not as a statistically accurate tool for overall planning. Volunteers proved to be very useful in providing assistance to the relocatees. A major part of the project's effort was devoted to informing individuals of their rights and intervening between clients and public agencies, to expedite their receipt of benefits in the face of confusion in policies and bureaucratic delays.

The Providence project examined the impact of relocation on the functioning of individuals and the social services best designed to assuage this impact. It brought to the fore the harmful social consequences of displacement and the sensitivity and patience required in dealing with older persons. Neighborhood social service centers were recommended as a major means of improving service to the elderly, and the importance of a continuing contact, sometimes long after the move has taken place, was stressed.

The four projects, taken together, raise at least eight important points. The most serious of these is the failure of even the best community welfare systems to reach many of the persons in critical need. Unclear objectives and poor interagency communications are seen as two primary causes for this inadequacy. A second is the need for a great deal more low-cost housing, and particularly public housing for the elderly. Third is the need for broadening the role of the relocation agency, so as to assure that the most critical problems of the relocatees are met. A fourth matter is that of the prerelocation period, which is vital to successful relocation and wherein a close worker-client relationship can be achieved and latent needs can be illuminated. Centralization, both in bringing responsibility for all relocation services under the umbrella of one agency and in the internal administration of an agency, is a necessary administrative step. Volunteer workers are seen as extremely useful in providing practical assistance and easing the load of overburdened caseworkers. Finally, friendly visiting, church centers, interagency training programs, neighborhood social service centers, and, on occasion, citizen review boards are positive suggestions of ways to institutionalize the valuable services temporarily provided by the demonstration projects. While all of these improvements can add to the success of a relocation program, however, they can hardly insure success. The pages that follow will elaborate on how a much higher level of performance might be attained.

5

TOWARD A PROGRAM OF POSITIVE RELOCATION

Relocation is a field which is at one and the same time very narrow and very broad. Viewed in the programmatic context within which it has heretofore operated, it is a somewhat constricted set of procedures carried out more as a necessity rather than being used as a tool to achieve specific social goals. Yet viewed in a larger sense, it touches a number of housing and social issues which have a direct bearing on the well-being of many families and individuals. It is in this larger context that the program must be viewed if we are to benefit from the experience of relocation and if we are to discover a proper role for relocation in the processes of urban redevelopment and social welfare reform. This chapter addresses itself first, therefore, to the broad implications of the research, and only second to the more practical and immediate considerations that demand attention.

THE REDEVELOPMENT PROGRAM

Two decades of relocation under urban renewal and other redevelopment programs have dramatized two very important facts. First, a city's desire to adapt to the forces produced by a changing society cannot be brought to fulfillment if the terms of reference are limited to land economics and esthetics. In many ways, our preoccupation with immediate improvements in such things as the economic base, urban efficiency, and visual attractiveness has preempted the possibility of serving directly the neediest sectors of our urban population. What is more, the political awakening to the obvious inequity and even injustice that this preoccupation has occasioned has recently restrained the city from making many of the physical improvements that are so obviously necessary.

The act has been not so much one of commission, but of omission. As has been pointed out elsewhere, the cause of this potential stalemate is not so much the often alleged immorality of the programs that seek to adapt the city's land use to changing technology, tastes, and spatial relationships, but rather the immorality of not serving the needs of the changing urban population as well. That is, while it is a legitimate function of government to improve a city's physical and economic conditions, it is also the responsibility of government to rectify imbalances and remove inequities, to say nothing of not itself adding to the problem. The current public irritation with clearance and relocation is symptomatic of the dissatisfaction with the balance that has been struck between these two functions. Redevelopment without adequate rehousing hardly seems like a fair exchange.

The second fact is that, despite its subservient position, relocation has in many cities moved a great distance toward a point where it can be of real service to the people it affects, while the burdens it imposes are minimized by an empathetic and responsible relocation staff. Even in the best relocation programs, of course, success is hardly universal, because of the overriding importance of basic and long-standing human and social problems and the limitations on the degree to which the relocation agent can effect changes in the housing market or the larger social system.

Thus it is concluded here that relocation has matured since the early 1950's, and has indeed begun to contribute in important ways to the body of knowledge in the field of social welfare. Redevelopment policy, meanwhile, has leaned much too far away from equity considerations and has thereby inhibited much of the creative work that would otherwise have been possible, and has generated a public reaction that has begun to inhibit physical renewal itself.

The response at this critical stage has not been altogether negative. The Model Cities legislation, for example, is built upon principles of equitable redistribution. Its precursors, the Workable Program and the Community Renewal Program, were similarly motivated. Likewise, the growth of the Department of Health, Education, and Welfare, the declaration of a war on poverty, and the establishment of a Department of Housing and Urban De-

velopment all signify in part a national recognition of the rights
and needs of the urban poor. Nevertheless, the appropriations for
these programs have thus far been hardly commensurate with the
rhetoric of the legislation. Not only is the money inadequate for
the tasks at hand, but the appropriations are unnecessarily parsi-
monious considering the abundance enjoyed by the population as
a whole.

Implications for Renewal and Relocation

In the absence of a rehousing component in the urban renewal
program, the relocation program has in many ways attempted to
fill the gap. Local relocation agencies, for example, often take the
responsibility for all displacement occasioned by clearance programs. Many offer rehousing services to families living in units
that are in violation of the local housing code. Some have begun
to aid welfare recipients, who often constitute the bulk of inade-
quately housed families. Although relocation agents have no direct
control over the housing supply, cooperation with public housing
authorities has been encouraged by federal regulations, and it is
not unusual for relocation agencies to institute rent supplement
schemes or other devices to expand their clients' housing opportunities. In dealing with entire households in a helpful manner, these
efforts have often resulted in the resolution of housing-related
problems and other deprivations. The experience gained and the
concern exhibited by the best relocation agencies would thus indicate that they are in a position to be given substantial power and
responsibility in any effort that might be mounted to achieve the
principal goal of the Housing Act of 1949—that every household
should be properly housed in a decent environment.

With these gains in understanding and practice, the greatest
handicap which these relocation agencies now have is the universal shortage of low-rent, decent housing. It is, indeed, this continuing shortage which at bottom forced the development of governmental relocation services. Such a supply is of course not sufficient
in itself. A growing, evolving society will always generate some
involuntary dislodgement, and even with an available choice of
vacant dwellings, a just and humane relocation program would
have to provide assistance beyond that of a simple real estate
agent. Nevertheless, at this time, the greatest gain in amelioration

of the difficulties of relocation of the elderly, as of all other relocatees, lies in the provision of such housing in adequate amounts.

No city has achieved this goal during the two decades since it became the nation's avowed policy. Although the renewal program has already begun to change, an intensification of efforts in this direction is clearly called for. In this context, however, it must be stated that it is not necessary to deny the validity of renewal programs aimed at changing land uses, in order to stress the importance of including provision of low-cost housing among the land uses with urgent priority. Indeed, it is only when sufficient progress has been made toward creating a supply of housing commensurate with the need that it will be morally and politically feasible again to determine the appropriate treatment for any neighborhood, whether it be improvement of its housing or supersession of the residential use, in accordance with overall city requirements. If the renewal program so changes its direction, relocation itself must be transformed from a service whose primary goal is movement of people out of their present houses to enable them to be demolished or rehabilitated, to a service whose goal is the rehousing of poorly housed people. Such an expanded program should contain the following elements:

1. An explicit statement that adequate housing of low-income households is a prime purpose of urban redevelopment. Renewal aimed at changing land uses might be continued, but renewal designed to increase the housing opportunities open to the poor and to provide them with an environment that is supportive rather than retarding would also be aggressively initiated and carried forth on a scale commensurate with the urgency of the task.

2. Expansion of other housing programs, including interest-rate subsidies, rent supplements, code enforcement, and particularly public housing in its advanced and innovative forms, that serve the more impoverished sectors of the population and that operate in a scattered fashion over wide areas of the city and metropolitan region. These programs currently should be bolstered to provide housing at a rate at least equivalent to the net loss in low-cost units resulting from the total urban redevelopment effort.

3. Rehousing services to all households displaced by urban renewal or by any other public action. These services should resemble the best of the current relocation programs, complete with site

offices and the whole range of housing and housing-related aids.
4. *Rehousing services to all low-income or otherwise disadvantaged households who presently reside in substandard or inappropriate dwellings, irrespective of whether they live in an area scheduled for redevelopment. These services should be a continuing part of a larger neighborhood assistance program, which also might include legal aid, consumer education, and other elements of a neighborhood service center.*
5. *Gradual development of a rationale for the proper location of housing for one subpopulation, as compared with another, on grounds of their comparative tastes and needs for accessibility, convenience, living space, and other amenities. An effort such as this, to record and evaluate the success of individual rehousing cases, would in time lead to development of an extended cost-benefit calculus in which maximization of land values is but one component. It might even be that, with this tool, certain areas now occupied by middle or upper-income households would be designated as renewal areas in order to provide lower-income households with better housing in a more suitable location. Such a possibility seems far-fetched today only because the traditional emphasis has been quite the opposite.*

A program which encompassed these five elements would of necessity have to be controlled by the equivalent of a local Centralized Housing Service, in which today's relocation specialist would play a central role. Centralized direction of this type would enable the program to benefit from the experience already gained by relocation workers. It would also insure cooperative planning among all major agencies engaged in the delivery of housing services and related services to the less affluent members of the community. It would bring about a speedier response to changing market conditions, and would tend to change the low-cost supply from a sellers' market to a buyers' market. As a consequence, it would remake the image of public redevelopment from that of a bulldozer to that of a housebuilder.

The likely alternative to revisions such as those outlined above is a continuation of the resistance to physical redevelopment, an inhibition to adaptive change, and a persistence of the housing problems that have plagued our cities long beyond a reasonable period of time.

RELOCATION POLICY QUESTIONS

The suggested transformation of the relocation agency into a re-housing service, in conjunction with changed priorities in the urban renewal program itself, necessarily would take years to accomplish. In view of the tremendous differences in the quality of current relocation agencies, it can be taken for granted that, even with federal encouragement, cities would vary in the pace and extent to which they adopted these goals and accomplished these changes. Meanwhile, there are policy, administrative, and procedural changes which would materially improve today's relocation programs and that are of immediate concern to agency personnel. Many of these would continue to be applicable even after adoption of the more fundamental approach outlined above.

There is general agreement that a person forced to relocate should not be expected to bear any needless burden for that action. There is further a growing belief, which has found support in this inquiry, that this negative approach should be modified and that relocation should be used as an opportunity to make a positive contribution to the lives of the impoverished urban households it frequently affects. The following pages will provide some suggestions as to how these principles may be implemented. They will deal with such broadly based issues as decent housing for all Americans and racial integration, as well as such specific concerns as financial assistance to relocatees and uniform relocation benefits. They are presented within the context of renewal as it is known today, with the full knowledge that these suggestions are an essential part of but hardly a substitute for the five-point program suggested in the previous section.

Housing

Even without a fundamental transformation in program, more can be done to provide an adequate rehousing supply which is, of course, the *sine qua non* of successful relocation. Current HUD requirements for relocation housing are more stringent and more strictly enforced than at any previous time in the urban renewal program. Localities receive approval for renewal projects that will cause displacement only after they provide detailed numerical evidence that there is enough decent, safe, and sanitary housing to rehouse the dislodged residents, or that it will be provided.

But the recitation of data on current and expected vacancies in the existing stock or of units under construction to meet general housing demand hardly guarantees that the individual needs of each household will in fact be met. Furthermore, unless secured or reserved by the relocation agency, a unit documented as vacant at the time of the survey may be occupied by the time displacement actually occurs.

What is required, then, is that renewal be accompanied by the construction or rehabilitation of sufficient private and public housing on or off the site, which is directly responsive to the needs and financial capabilities of those being displaced. The provision of such housing should be a key ingredient in renewal plans and should be timed to coincide with displacement activities. In fact, in no case should displacement be allowed to occur until appropriate replacement housing is available. Then, when it is ready, project residents should be granted unchallenged first preference for occupancy, and should be supported with rent supplements and whatever other assistance may exist to improve their position in the housing market.

As desirable as it appears to have a housing program parallel displacement activities, it is nevertheless not feasible to impose a strict federal mandate for equivalent replacement, which would require a new unit to be constructed for every unit demolished. The availability of standard housing in satisfactory neighborhoods no doubt varies from city to city, and the localities should be given leeway in formulating their housing programs. But in all cases where the existing housing supply is utilized as a relocation resource, due consideration should be given to the constricting effect such a course of action will have upon the housing market, especially in the low-rent sector. In fact, if localities judge every renewal project on the basis of its total impact on the housing situation of low and moderate-income households, and then take the appropriate steps toward providing the needed housing, the cry against unjust or improper relocation would be largely abated.

For many displaced households, public housing represents the only chance for decent living arrangements. Public housing construction has increased in recent years, and the increase has benefited elderly households primarily. About one-half of recently constructed units have been intended solely for the elderly. The demonstration projects have confirmed the fact that where such housing has been built with attendant social and health services and has been in a suitable location, the response has been enthusiastic. Since the elderly are in greatest need, this allocation may not be unreasonable. Regardless of whether the general public housing program is expanded, accelerated construction of units for the elderly is obviously desirable.

Attention to certain modifications in the public housing program as a whole will be necessary, however, before we can say with equal confidence that the program for younger households should be as rapidly expanded. For example, many households in greatest need and who thereby deserve priority, are ineligible under existing regulations. Among them are large families, single persons, households with incomes so low as to place them beneath the minimum effective income levels allowable in public housing, and households normally considered to be socially unacceptable as tenants. Another matter is that of the flexibility and responsiveness of the program. Recent innovations such as leasing of private homes, rent-purchase agreements, "turnkey" schemes, and especially scattered-site developments, should become major components of the public housing program, and additional modifications should be developed. The public housing program could thus take on new life by extending its central role as a provider of adequate housing for the families and individuals who are unable to compete effectively in the private market.

Public housing should not be expected to carry the entire burden, however. In order to insure that the production of high quality units for low-income persons is maximized, increased effort must be directed toward prodding and assisting the private market. The enforcement of local housing codes is basic to the success of a comprehensive attack on the housing problem. Equally necessary are programs to improve the demand position of households of modest income. Interest-free rehabilitation loans, subsidized mortgage interest rates, rent supplements, and housing information services are useful in this regard, and all should be adequately funded so that they can be put into play wherever the need dictates. In addition, the housing industry should be served with up-to-date local demand analyses and should be informed of redevelopment plans and opportunities to serve special groups so that it can become an integral part of the city's comprehensive rehousing effort. Recent proposals for special tax incentives for rental housing and mortgage terms for cooperatives are worthy of thorough consideration.

In the case of the younger family, it is essential to provide opportunities not only to rent but also to own. Present welfare policies, public housing regulations, mortgage-lending practices, and other devices systematically and unreasonably restrict the low-income family from buying its own home. The economic advantages and symbolic values of home ownership are effectively placed beyond the reach of the very groups that so desperately need them in order to become fully independent and fully responsible citizens. Such programs as Section 221 (h) of the Housing Act of 1966 should thus receive the aggressive attention of relocation officials, and no opportunity for ownership should be arbitrarily excluded from the range of options open to the relocation client.

In the case of the elderly, the federal programs that have demonstrated the greatest possibility of success and that tend to serve the most pressing housing and related needs are the 202, the 221 (d) (3), the 231 and the nursing home programs, which have been described in Chapter 2. These and other similar federal and state programs already serve substantial numbers of older Americans, and with the use of rent supplements on a broad scale, they could be instrumental in overcoming many of the deficiencies that have been exposed herein.

A final point of importance has to do with the size of the area whose housing is being considered as a relocation resource. Considering the shift of job and other opportunities from city to suburbs, the metropolitan region as a whole is the only proper basis for relocation planning. Realistically, it will be some time before effective regional cooperation on housing matters can be achieved, but the goal is worth whatever effort can be applied toward its achievement. As a first step, it should become common practice to maintain up-to-date vacancy information for all types of housing in the region, and the preparation of a real property inventory, whereby all structures in the region would be registered and changes in each structure, its value or rent, and its occupancy would automatically be recorded, is not too much to expect in a few years. Many regional planning bodies are even now in a position to promote knowledge about the region's housing market, and they should begin to operate as an ally of renewal and relocation agencies. Relocation from central cities to suburban areas or even planned new towns could be effectively geared to new employment opportunities. It would then resemble the resettlement schemes of World War II which were successful precisely because they were oriented toward employment rather than rehousing alone.

Desegregation in Housing

Militating against regional housing considerations and successful relocation in general is the continuing discrimination against Negroes and members of other minority groups in the housing market, coupled with the current reluctance of many such persons to subject themselves to the isolation and abuse that the white suburb represents to them. It is particularly difficult to utilize a large portion of the housing stock in relocation because of the absence of rent or income subsidies sufficiently large to offset the poverty so general among relocatees, but the presence of active discrimination in the market exacerbates this situation several times over.

Besides limiting choices of residential location, discrimination also limits the range of housing types that are open to relocatees. Perhaps even more important, it serves to sustain the artificially high prices of housing in areas that are open to minority residence.

It hardly need be said that a relocation effort should attempt to satisfy the entire package of housing needs and desires of each of its clients, with total disregard of patterns of segregation, except insofar as the client himself is concerned with them. Furthermore, a reasonable subsidy should be allowed toward the goal of satisfying these individual preferences. It is not possible, on the other hand, for the relocation agent to have very much direct control over the patterns of segregation themselves and the instrumentalities that reinforce them, such as real estate and financial interests.

Of particular importance to this study is the degree to which a reluctant elderly relocatee should be asked to be the pioneer in promoting racial integration. By and large, older relocatees have a greater need for familiar surroundings than do most younger families. To ask them to face the initial trials of integration in addition to the encroaching problems of old age and adjustment to a new home and neighborhood is to ask them to participate in an innovation which can be more easily carried on by younger, more adaptable households. At the same time, relocation of several willing persons into one area might provide them with sufficient support to make such a move desirable.

Financial Assistance

In order to elevate relocation into a positive program, there must be instituted more generous and imaginative systems of financial assistance to displaced households and businesses than presently exists. This assistance should be a real inducement to the relocatee rather than a modest compensation for his trouble. Furthermore, the administration of the system should be as simple and straightforward as possible, and should avoid the stigma associated with "means tests" and other symbols of public dependency.

Just compensation to the owner occupant should, then, include more than the fair market value for his home or property and the payment of moving and other incidental costs. There should be provided an additional payment, designed to act as an incentive to quicker and more satisfactory relocation, reduce the degree to which the relocation agency must provide real estate and other services, and modify or even eliminate much of what now appear to be social casework problems. The injection of extra cash could even buttress some of the most impoverished households and lessen the likelihood that they would continue in the state of deprivation that preceded relocation.

This payment should be made as a lump sum, based on a fixed schedule, rather than being based on an investigation of the actual costs incurred in each case. Such payments are now permitted to a limited degree. They have many advantages, not the least of which are the reduction in bureaucratic delays, the uniformity of administrative practice, and the expediting of the move itself.

In this connection, it is distressing to note the caution and petty morality that are involved in much administrative practice. Great care and public expense seem to be taken to prevent any "cheating" on the part of the client. This is true not only of relocation, of course, but of many other public programs involving the individual household. In a court of justice, great care and expense is often taken to prevent the innocent from being found guilty, and our society is willing to accept the fact that in the process some guilty parties will go free. It is anomalous that in relocation, and in public welfare practices generally, the concern seems to be that no "guilty" party should go undetected, even though this attitude assures that a great many innocent parties will receive inadequate and inequitable treatment. Lump sum payments are one means of correcting this injustice.

Quite apart from the level of payments and the manner in which they are administered is the matter of proper timing. Payment should be made as early in the renewal process as possible. If the relocation agency is prepared to set its service apparatus in motion and is assured that vacated rental units scheduled for clearance will not be reinhabited, payments should be allowed as early as the survey and planning stage of renewal. To prevent inequity, this may carry with it the necessity for early acquisition. A risk in such a procedure is that renewal plans for the area may be altered, but this possibility is usually quite remote. In order to facilitate moves timed to the desires of the relocatees themselves, then, the federal government should loosen the current regulations which usually do not allow federal money for relocation payments until the loan and grant contract for renewal is approved.

Finally, in addition to an increase in present benefits, the overall program of financial aids should be broadened and made more responsive to the specific financial needs of sectors of the population that suffer uncommon hardships. Among the elderly, for example, this means that displaced homeowners seeking to purchase new housing should be given greater federal financial assistance in securing new mortgages; that the workers who lose their job because of displacement of either their residence or place of work should be given special unemployment compensation benefits; that small businessmen adversely affected but not displaced by renewal should be given some remuneration as well as the opportunity for low-interest loans; that displaced, tenant small businessmen should be entitled to government-guaranteed leases if they seek to rent property again or low-interest loans if they seek to buy property; and that displaced small businessmen, because of such factors as outdated skills and lack of seniority, should be considered "elderly" at the age of 55 or even 50, and be given greater assistance, along with those over 62 years old, in obtaining the working capital needed to start a new business.

Uniform Relocation Benefits

A fourth broad policy area that still requires attention is that of the comparative treatment given to relocatees in similar circumstances but displaced by different programs. While relocation caused by urban renewal is still far from perfect, for example, its concern for its clients has increased, whereas the federal highway program as yet has paid little heed to the needs of the persons it has displaced. The need for equal treatment is widely recognized, and some steps have been taken in the direction of equalizing the benefits and services offered to all relocatees. Adoption of this policy must be completed, with application to all programs at all governmental levels.

CONDUCTING A POSITIVE PROGRAM OF SERVICE

While high-level policy decisions will have a significant bearing on the future course of relocation, there are a great many more detailed matters which, to the relocatee himself, are equally as crucial. These are related to the anxieties and discomforts experienced by persons in preparing themselves for relocation, in actually moving, and in adjusting to a new environment. This section discusses what the local relocation agency can itself do to mitigate these disruptive effects of relocation and to turn its program into one of positive human service.

At the first serious indication of redevelopment in a given area, the relocation service apparatus should be set in motion. As information is obtained on the needs and characteristics of the people in the area, plans should be developed for the extent and type of services to be offered. In most cases, the relocation agency should be prepared to provide services from at least one and one-half years before property acquisition to at least one and one-half years after relocation. This period of time is not, of course, necessary in all cases, but it is often essential in working with elderly clients, where time and patience are needed in building up a relationship of trust and easing the delicate process of adjustment.

Interagency Coordination

A successful rehousing service program requires the dedication of the entire complement of public and private agencies which constitute a community's social service network. To gain this, the relocation agency should take an aggressive role in enlisting their participation early in the planning stage. There are many vehicles for effecting the cooperation that is so obviously necessary. One example of these is the interagency conference, which can serve as a means of informing the service agencies of displacement plans and goals of relocation, and can in turn educate the relocation agent to the services the community agencies have to offer. This might take the form of a training seminar, as in the San Antonio demonstration. Where gaps are found and commitments cannot be obtained, of course, the relocation agency should itself make the effort to provide the necessary services.

Establishment of a Site Office

Most cities have by now discovered the desirability of establishing a site office in each redevelopment area well before clearance or other action actually takes place. There, information and advice can be easily dispensed, relationships with the community can be established, and the relocatees can place their move in a context and learn of the rights and opportunities associated with relocation. If the antipoverty program has established a neighborhood service center, the site office would properly be located there.

Generally unrecognized is the fact that the site office can be a means of promoting a sense of community and stability among the relocatees, concerns of paramount importance to older persons. Where new housing is to be built on the cleared land or close to the project itself, the site office could serve as a rental office to register the households desiring to remain in the neighborhood. If a large number of households relocate in the same neighborhood, a site office in the receiving area could serve to bolster postrelocation services.

Initial Contact with Site Residents

As in the case of any social service program, the nature of the relationship with the client is vital. Relocation workers must be trained to be fully sympathetic to the needs of those being displaced. The initial contact with site residents should reflect respect for the client's rights and dignity. The relocation worker should arrange with the client to visit at a convenient time, preferably through a telephone call, or if that is not possible, through a note written in plain language. He should attempt to talk to the head of the household, even if that necessitates a night or weekend visit. This first visit—and most of those that follow as well—should be made with individual households. Group interviews are hardly sufficient to announce public decisions that will affect a household in very intimate ways. This is especially true of elderly persons, who often find it difficult to communicate in a group meeting and need personal reassurances.

The first interview should be unstructured, designed to give information and allay fears rather than to gather detailed information. Assurance of the family's rights and the relocation agency's determination to respect them will eliminate much of the needless confusion and anxiety so often experienced upon relocation.

The most effective communication at this stage is face-to-face exchange, but the interviewer could leave a fact sheet, specifically listing the benefits to which the client is entitled and other pertinent information, such as the location and working hours of the site office. The worker should also leave a calling card informing the client where and at what times he may be reached if help is needed.

The relocation agency should be prepared to follow up this initial contact with immediate service. There should be no limit on the number of visits, which should be made often enough in each case to provide the full range of available services. To make clients more receptive to help, the relocation agency should assure them a degree of continuity by having the same worker visit them on most occasions and by attempting to limit the number of other agency personnel with whom they must deal.

Diagnostic Survey

Shortly after the initial interview, a diagnostic survey of the site residents should be conducted, by or under the auspices of the relocation agency. The intent of the survey should be to identify only the most relevant factors about the respondents. Such surveys often lose their focus and deal more with peripheral than central issues. This pitfall should be avoided and every effort made to use the survey as a quick appraisal of the human condition, geared to mobilizing immediate services in the amounts necessary to deal with the problems at hand. It should focus on specific subgroups of the relocation population and attempt to determine their characteristic needs. The single elderly male and the elderly widow, for example, are overrepresented in the relocation caseloads and often have easily identifiable needs. The goal of the survey should be to isolate these needs and then to fashion a program of service based on them specifically. A tenant profile card, capsulizing the client's important social, financial, and health needs along with his relocation desires, can facilitate such an appraisal.

Counseling and Referral Services

The relocation worker has the unique opportunity of dealing with the important internal relationships of the entire household and with its relationships to its social and physical environment as well. In such a situation, opportunities for service are great, but the responsibility demands a degree of professional competence beyond that possessed by most workers. The need for sensitive and speedy referral is thus obvious.

The possibility of referring a client to another agency may, however, often inadvertently encourage mediocre initial service. Relocation is a period of crisis, and to be able to deal effectively with problems as they appear, the relocation worker himself must be trained to take responsibility and initiative. That is, it is incumbent upon the agency itself to offer a certain amount of casework service. The long-term objective is, of course, to transfer responsibility to the appropriate agencies, but for the short term, the relocation agency itself should be prepared to provide social work assistance to both the household and to its individual members as problems arise.

Where a referral is made, the relocation worker should still maintain contact, to see if the relocatee followed through on the referral and to determine if additional help is needed. Admittedly, only a few relocation agencies now have the resources necessary to offer such extensive casework or referral services. Yet their assumption of the responsibility for comprehensive treatment and assistance, either directly or indirectly through contracts with other agencies, is clearly necessary if relocation is to move in a forward direction.

For elderly relocatees, the case for extensive social work assistance is an especially strong one. Even without relocation, the plagues of loneliness, insecurity, ill health, and low income present difficult problems with which the elderly clients and workers assisting them must cope. With relocation, these problems can be transformed into major personal crises, requiring the closest possible contact and communication between the older person and the social service workers.

Housing Assistance

The relocation agency should be actively engaged in finding housing in the existing stock which is appropriate to the needs of its clients. A number of avenues have been used by various agencies which have not yet been widely adopted and of which many agencies may be unaware. Finder's fees may be useful in finding units for very large households and others whose competitive position in the housing market is weak. FHA or VA-acquired properties may be available for sale or rent. Building permits can be checked to determine new construction. Telephone and utility companies and mail carriers can inform the agency of vacancies. An up-to-date listing of all sale and rental dwellings found through such means, including rental housing units under construction, should be readily available at the site offices. The agency should encourage multiple listings of rental vacancies by real estate agents similar to those for sales properties. The relocation worker should inform households individually of the housing available, and of rent supplements and other devices intended to serve their housing needs.

Many persons who must relocate are entirely competent and willing to find new housing themselves. For such households, referrals equivalent to those made by real estate agents may be sufficient assistance. Others, particularly among the elderly, may need far more help. For them, the relocation agency's responsibility should, in addition, extend to help in inspecting the housing that is available. At the least, the relocation worker should arrange for a meeting at a specific time between the landlord or agent and the household, and should provide explicit directions on how to reach the meeting place. While not losing sight of the fact that people often gain more satisfaction from their rehousing if they feel they have found it themselves, the worker might also accompany the homeseeker and help him evaluate a dwelling's overall suitability to his needs. To the elderly, for example, the environment and convenience of neighborhood facilities, in addition to the housing unit itself, are of prime importance and careful guidance in considering their adequacy would be most helpful.

Some displaced households find it difficult to obtain appropriate housing because they do not satisfy the criteria of social acceptability established by the landlord or public housing authority. In some borderline cases, the relocation worker might be able to support the eligibility of his clients, or if they are clearly ineligible, to make a special appeal on their behalf.

Once a household has selected a new home, the agency should be ready to help with the moving and settling chores. If necessary, it should help the household find a mover. The best choice is often a small neighborhood mover, who is used to handling small loads and is usually flexible in making arrangements. On moving day, it is often beneficial to have a helper, perhaps a volunteer, assist the elderly households with the many small physical tasks and decisions involved in resettlement. It is also worthwhile to have a worker or volunteer on hand to greet the displaced household upon arrival at its new home, providing emotional support as well as practical information.

Social and Psychological Assistance

It is clear by now that elderly persons depend greatly on their immediate environment for their social and psychological well being. This study has sought to elucidate their environmental needs so that the relocation agency might be on firmer ground than in the past in helping elderly households select and adjust to a new housing situation. Gaps in our understanding still exist, to be sure, but the following statements on environmental needs of the elderly appear to be generally valid and should be taken into consideration in any relocation service program: (1) Many elderly persons prefer to live in the immediate company of others of the same age, but do not wish to be altogether removed from the presence of younger persons. (2) It is important for the elderly to live in an area where there is peace and quiet but which has access to a diversity of activity. (3) It is desirable to have a focal point of activity where friendships can be made easily, inconspicuously, and informally. (4) Older persons enjoy paying frequent, short visits to their families, but often prefer not to live so close as to become continually involved. (5) There must be public transportation available in the immediate vicinity. (6) Grocery stores and drug stores should be within one or two blocks. (7) Hospital clinics, banks, and churches should be close by, though not necessarily within walking distance. (8) Residence on the fringe of the central business district or other centers of activity is often the most desirable location for senior citizen housing.

In order to hasten the elderly household's integration into a new neighborhood, the relocation agency should make sure that the necessary postrelocation aids are available. Settlement houses, church groups, golden age clubs, and other social organizations in the receiving neighborhood should be informed of the new elderly residents' arrival and encouraged to contact them. Also, with some imagination, adjustment can be made less painful. For instance, a map of the new neighborhood, showing the location of important facilities, such as drug stores, grocery stores, bus stops, and churches, would serve a useful purpose. Similarly, a calendar of social events in the area would help familiarize the newcomers with their surroundings.

As yet, group relocation has only been used occasionally as a means of preserving social stability upon displacement. We have seen, especially in strongly ethnic areas, that elderly households are often highly dependent on neighboring households or places of business. Where possible, then, the relocation agency should be sympathetic to these symbiotic relationships and should attempt to preserve them. For example, it should help the managers of displaced buildings, which housed many long-term tenants, find other suitable facilities in which many of the same tenants might be relocated. It should encourage private organizations to develop or support accommodations for groups of displaced households. And, where a substantial number of households from the project area relocate in the same neighborhood, it should encourage certain organizations and businesses from the project area to reestablish in that same receiving neighborhood. To be successful, such efforts require the participation and support of other community agencies, but here, as in other cases, the relocation agency can take the initiative.

Income Assistance

Aside from granting the full extent of relocation payments allowable in each case, it is not the function of the relocation agency to provide direct financial assistance. Yet indirectly, the agency's efforts can have significant financial implications for its clients. Assistance in achieving satisfactory housing and environmental conditions can lead to real economies and reduce the costs that would be created by inadequate surroundings. As an obvious example, a person relocated within walking distance of frequently used facilities is saved the expense of transportation.

In addition, the counseling and referral services of the agency can often help relocatees make better use of their limited financial resources, and it is not unusual for a worker to discover that a relocatee is entitled to but not receiving monetary income from OAA, OASDI, or some other source. In these cases, a relocation worker who is familiar with the intricacies of income maintenance programs can play a vital role in improving a household's financial status.

Health Assistance

In regard to health there is even less direct assistance that can be given by the relocation agency. As in the case of income, the health benefits that accrue will be largely dependent on the quality of housing and social service provided. In fact, since there is some evidence that a forced move may increase the mortality rate of older persons, the caliber of these services may in some cases be a matter of life or death.

Sensitive counseling and referral services are thus important in promoting the health of displaced, elderly households. The relocation agency should form a close and active liaison with the district health association, community health centers, and whatever other appropriate health resources may exist in the community. These organizations should be informed of the health problems found during relocation and encouraged to take part in the service program, and, conversely, the relocatee should be encouraged to make use of these facilities. Here again, though, the agency's responsibility does not terminate once the referral is made, since counsel is still often needed by the households. For example, in a case where referral has led to a physician's decision that institutionalization is necessary, the relocation worker should comfort the person and his family, and help them implement the decision.

Elderly Small Businessmen

The problems faced by the displaced resident are usually quite serious; for the elderly businessman they can be devastating. Thus it is that special attention should be given to these persons, and the services that are provided must be tailor-made to each particular case.

Consultation, preferably expert consultation, is the basic ingredient, regardless of the specific needs involved. The procedural complexities that the small businessman must face during displacement and reestablishment make advisory assistance particularly crucial to him. He should be informed, both by visit and through written materials, of the assistance that the Small Business Administration has to offer, of the sites at which he might reestablish his business, of the financial recompense to which he is entitled, and of alternative employment he might choose. He should be given guidance on the provisions of the available federal loan programs and how he can apply for them. Where it appears feasible, a group of displaced small businessmen, elderly and non-elderly, should even be encouraged and assisted to form a corporation, with the purpose of relocating together in a shopping center or some other central point of activity.

Public Information

Finally, it should be emphasized that it is vital that both clients and the community as a whole receive accurate, complete information on the activities of the relocation service program. There is no substitute for the provision of real help through sincere and understanding personal contact in dealing with clients. But the relocation agency can take many additional, imaginative steps to foster a positive response among them. A useful device is a newsletter distributed periodically to site residents. Such a bulletin can be of great assistance in keeping households and businesses informed of renewal plans, clarifying relocation rights and assistance available, and generally curtailing false rumors which often plague relocation efforts.

Cordial relationships with clients no doubt play a key role in enhancing the community-wide image of relocation. An extensive publicity program can, however, promote this larger objective even further. News media can and should be utilized to advertise the human gains to be achieved through comprehensive relocation programs. Special programs conducted for elderly persons and other disadvantaged groups should be well publicized. Much of the responsibility in these matters rests with the relocation director, who most frequently represents the agency before civic groups and the general public. Effective communication is a crucial facet of any service program, and the relocation agency should use all the means at its disposal to achieve recognition and support.

ADMINISTRATION AND ORGANIZATION OF THE RELOCATION AGENCY

To carry out the comprehensive service program outlined in the foregoing sections, relocation agencies must fashion the necessary administrative apparatus. The specific administrative and organizational structure desirable in each locality will, of course, be influenced by the nature of local needs, institutions, and capabilities, as well as by the pace of redevelopment. For example, agencies in larger cities will probably be able to have larger staffs and provide more services directly than those in smaller cities. Yet while discrepancies of this sort are bound to exist, our inquiry has revealed a structural format which has general applicability.

Centralized Relocation Agency

One of the most important steps in strengthening the relocation machinery at the local level is the establishment of a centralized relocation agency, handling all governmentally induced displacement on a contract basis for agencies within the city and perhaps even in smaller, neighboring cities. It might even be charged with the responsibility of providing rehousing and housing-related social services to any poorly housed low-income, or otherwise handicapped household seeking to improve its living conditions, regardless of whether its current residence is within a redevelopment area.

This type of agency has a great many favorable things to be said for it. By simplifying contact with other agencies, better coordination and timing of displacement programs can be achieved. Highly qualified personnel can be recruited more easily and a greater degree of relocation competence can be developed. Greater visibility of the relocation responsibility can promote community support. Administrative chores can be reduced, as economies of scale are achieved. Caseloads can be stabilized. Record-keeping can be improved. And perhaps most important, uniform relocation practices can be advanced.

The concept of a centralized service agency has not yet been fully accepted. The vested interests of particular clearance programs often fear that their initiative will be thwarted, and it has been debated whether a "proper" displacement rate can in fact be established. These criticisms notwithstanding, the centralized agency stands as a hopeful means of unifying local redevelopment and housing policy. As a city-wide housing policy board, or in conjunction with one, it could move the city far along in its search for rational and responsible development policy.

Advisory Committee

Each centralized relocation agency should have a city-wide advisory committee to assist it and generate support for its program. Project area residents should be well represented on such a committee, together with a broad variety of community interests, such as real estate, finance, labor, antipoverty and social service workers. Its members should concern themselves with the operation of the service program, how it may be improved, its long-range goals, the constraints which act upon it, necessary cooperation with other agencies, personnel matters, and other relevant subjects. To maintain the committee's support and interest, its recommendations must of course be considered by the agency and reflected in the service program whenever possible.

This committee should be a permanent board, with a stable membership core, operating in liaison with the centralized relocation agency. It should not be confused with the oft-suggested neighborhood relocation committee, which would operate within a given project area. Rather than such a committee, the conduct of relocation within an individual neighborhood might be better reviewed by local antipoverty committees, whose concerns are broader than those of relocation alone.

LOCATION OF THE RELOCATION AGENCY IN THE GOVERNMENTAL STRUCTURE

Since constructive relocation is an important public responsibility, it should be recognized as such by making it a visible arm of government. It should therefore be under the administrative direction of the executive head of the local government unit. When the relocation function is set up in this manner, it is easier to gain the assistance of other governmental agencies and to guide the program in a manner consistent with the needs of the relocatees and the community. Ideally, all agencies that are directly involved with development and housing policy should be integrated into a local housing and development unit, of which rehousing services would be a principal program.

Staffing

Whether the agency is a central housing service or simply a good relocation service, it requires a complement of able staff members drawn from many different fields. There must be a number of trained social workers who are capable of coping with the difficult human problems that will be faced and of guiding the field operations of other workers. In addition, the overall background of the agency's staff should reflect experience in geriatrics, vocational counseling, business and real estate, household management, public health, community relations, and the formation and evaluation of statistical records. Outside consultants might be relied upon for some of the more specialized services, but especially in the larger agencies the staff as a whole should be competent in most of the required fields. At the apex of the agency, the director, too, should be conversant in these fields and preferably have experience in social services as well as housing.

Given the present low status of the relocation function in the system of social welfare planning and physical development, it is no wonder that the recruitment of quality staff members is a difficult task. Yet there is a growing interest among the youth of our nation in work that involves service to others, and as relocation assumes more importance and promise, there is no reason to suppose that the recruitment job will be insurmountable. This is not meant, however, to denigrate the importance of aggressive recruitment, adequate salaries, and continuing training in assuring a staff of the necessary ability.

Record-Keeping

Along with the many other prerequisites for a far-reaching service program is the need for a comprehensive and sophisticated record-keeping system. It is, first of all, important to have on file relevant information on the needs and characteristics about individual households in the caseload. The records should also provide an overall picture of the relocatees, so that their general problems can be identified and housing and social programs of proper magnitude can be planned. Individualized service and guidance is not to be discouraged, but rather such personalized service should be bulwarked by more basic assistance, such as a program providing suitable housing for the relocation population. Statistical information summarizing the condition of an entire group can provide a sound basis for such programs, can be used to present to the public a clear picture of the services that relocation does or can perform, and can provide a basis for evaluation of the services actually given and means of their improvement.

Volunteers

The assistance of volunteers in dealing with clients can be of considerable benefit to a relocation agency staff. By relieving professional staff members of some of the more easily performed tasks, volunteers can enable them to concentrate on the more difficult chores. Furthermore, volunteers often attack their job with a zest and determination which can serve to elevate the spirit of elderly persons and others on the relocation workload.

Yet it must be remembered that volunteers, like most new recruits, need proper training. They, too, must be made responsible for their actions and equipped with the understanding needed to deal successfully with clients. Toward this end, they should be required to take part in a highly structured, professionally conducted training course. Here they should be taught the objectives of the service program, the nature and extent of their responsibility, and the most appropriate methods of assisting needy households. As a part of such courses, group sessions focused around the discussion of actual field experiences are particularly useful as a means of preparing the volunteers for the difficult human problems they will encounter. Through the use of material drawn from field experience, volunteers can formulate plans indicating how they would act in a particular situation and how they can provide maximum assistance without becoming overly involved with a client or going beyond their own areas of competence.

Once volunteers are in the field, they should remain under the continual supervision of experienced workers. In no case should they be allowed unilaterally to make referrals, to treat those with deep-seated emotional problems, or to assume entire responsibility for maintaining case records. On the other hand, there are many duties which volunteers can properly and successfully perform. They can motivate clients to accept and follow through on certain services. They can provide emotional support. They can identify pressing needs. And for older clients in particular, they can provide practical physical aids in such activities as shopping, housekeeping, or helping the relocatee find a home, move, and establish himself in his new environment.

MAKING USE OF EXPERIENCE GAINED

Relocation Handbook

A successful residential move is dependent on many practical factors: the time allowed for planning and preparation; the degree of knowledge of available alternatives; the motivations behind the move and the attitudes toward moving; the financial, health, and other capabilities of the household, and other matters specific to the household in question. While some of these are beyond the control of relocation officials, many others can be positively affected by the manner in which relocation programs are conducted. Since relocation was first instituted as a public program, a great deal of practical understanding has developed in individual agencies on how the relocation job can best be administered and conducted, but there has been relatively little effort made to catalogue the accumulated knowledge as a guide to other relocation agencies. It would, therefore, be most useful to prepare a national compendium of exemplary efforts in carrying out relocation. Because it could be developed fairly easily and would have immediate practical importance, official Washington should assign high priority to the preparation of such a document.

The relocation handbook, as the document might be called, would logically be divided in accordance with the administrative tasks that the local relocation agency must perform. Following each heading, summaries of experimental programs or successful current programs might be given, each description being accompanied by the address to which further inquiry should be directed. Among the questions implicit under the various headings would be the following:

How early should relocation planning begin?

What are the best ways to notify relocatees and explain the program?

How can interagency coordination best be achieved in the service program?

What information about the area and its inhabitants will be most useful during the relocation process?

What skills are necessary, and at what points in the process to insure reasonable success?

What type of personnel is needed on relocation staffs? How can they be recruited and trained?

What opportunities for service does relocation present?

What specific steps can be taken to ease the adjustment to a new environment?

What type of follow-up services should be administered?

How can volunteers be utilized to best advantage?

How can relocation services be administered to insure maximum efficiency consistent with human benefit?

What are the requirements of a comprehensive real estate service?

In what way can the relocatee be motivated to seek and get the best possible rehousing?

What serious problems are likely to be uncovered?

How can the agency deal with them? What are the most important agencies to which problems can be referred?

What importance has moving day itself, and how can it be made as pleasant as possible?

In what form should records be kept? How will they be useful later on?

While some of these questions have broader overtones, most of them are largely of a "cookbook" nature, and these should be answered in terms of experience.

Relocation Performance Audit

At the present time, no standards exist by which the success of a relocation program can be satisfactorily gauged. Beyond a few notions about specific physical conditions and generalities about location and environment, it is difficult to evaluate relocation efforts, particularly in regard to their impact on national housing goals. On the one hand, administrators often have tended to define success as what actually happened, and on the other hand, evaluators have sometimes tended toward excessive criticism and even cynicism instead of offering better ways of determining and achieving success.

It would, then, be helpful to establish a performance audit of the relocation operation which would compare a relocatee's overall situation after the forced move with that before displacement. Operating along the same lines of the General Accounting Office in Washington, this audit should be carried out by an independent group, perhaps a governmental agency but preferably a private research group or university, and should be administered on a periodic basis to a sample of relocatees.

The record-keeping procedures suggested earlier would be of much practical importance to the conduct of a performance audit. But on the whole, the audit should be more heavily concerned with actual results than with the frequently cited data found in administrative records. The auditing group should seek the relocatee's own reaction to such matters as the new environment, housing quality, and the cost of living, and should place great weight on each household's overall satisfaction with its postrelocation situation. While promoting a sound evaluation of relocation's success, such information could also add to our understanding of preferences and of how to perform housing and social services more adequately.

THE GROWING RESPONSIBILITY

Whether it be a comprehensive service program on the order of the one suggested at the outset of this chapter, or whether it be simply the improvement of relocation as we now know it, the success of rehousing will depend on the actions taken at the various government levels and by private groups that serve the public interest.

The Federal Role

The federal government led the way in relocation, despite its early desire to leave this function largely in the hands of the local jurisdiction. It has instituted a number of housing and social programs designed to ease the human impact of displacement. It has made adequate relocation a prerequisite of urban renewal programs. And it has assumed the full cost for relocation payments under urban renewal and public housing. In the process, however, it has established a great array of bureaucratic rules and regulations. These have led to cumbersome procedures which are expensive and annoying and which cause unreasonable delays in the relocation process.

It might, then, be useful to determine whether the relocation job can be done with far less federal regulation and more local independence than at present. A test situation might be established wherein a local board is empowered to make final judgments as to the observance of federal guidelines. The federal agencies themselves or an impartial body could then compare the results with those of other relocation programs carried out in the same city or elsewhere under the current system of extensive prior federal review. It may be that such a test case would show that the locality can bear the responsibility of fixing performance standards, in whole or in part, and for policing the program without violating the intent of the federal mandate. Of course, if performance audits are universally adopted, they might permit general relaxation of prior federal review, subject to reinstatement of controls in any community whose services were found to be below federal standards.

An area in which the federal government might profitably expand its influence is in the services offered by the regional offices of its agencies. These offices should provide a locality with more

extensive assistance during the formulation of renewal and relocation proposals, rather than leaving it solely up to the locality to
prove the validity of its proposals through detailed documentation.
Under the current *modus operandi* there is too much federal stress
on statistical presentations and too little concern with the actual
preparation and programming of plans. To pursue this proposal
logically, the regional offices should offer a full range of specialized services during the implementation of the plans. For the relocation agency, such an expanded service role by the regional
offices would mean a greater base of experience to draw upon in
handling the thorny problems that will inevitably arise during the
course of a service program.

The State's Responsibility

Urban renewal and relocation, like the low-rent public housing
program, have operated by means of a federal-local partnership, a
phenomenon which many observers feel will increasingly charac-
terize American federalism. State governments have generally
done little in the area of relocation other than provide localities
with the necessary statutory authority. A few states have assumed
a financial stake in the one-third local share of renewal costs, and
have thereby helped to pay for administration of relocation activities. Some have provided limited technical and advisory assistance
and some have even expanded eminent domain statutes in order to
provide those displaced by state and local programs with compensation more nearly equal to that given under urban renewal. But
the scope of all such activities has thus far been minimal.

Whatever one's disposition toward the proper role of the states
in our federal system, their resources can be added to those of the
federal government in such a way as to produce substantially
better results. This is particularly true in the smaller localities,
which are often hard-pressed to provide positive relocation services. State funds can help bolster the administrative capacity of
these agencies and can help finance some of the expensive components of the service program. In addition, state technical and advisory assistance can be instrumental in training relocation staffs
in ways of preparing and carrying out a comprehensive service
program and in promoting innovation in the performance of the
relocation function.

Local Government

While federal initiative and financial support are necessary to do the job, they alone are hardly sufficient. In the last analysis, it must be assumed that each local jurisdiction will act responsibly and that it knows best its own needs. Whether a centralized relocation agency is needed must thus be determined locally, and whether one is established and given extensive power will be a local decision. Whether a city-wide housing policy board, on which the relocation agency is given a high status, is formed, and whether it will be empowered to initiate the needed housing programs and to decide upon the rate at which various displacement activities may take place will rest on local commitment and local action. In the larger cities, the creation of departments of urban development concerned with the integration of housing, planning, code enforcement, and relocation activities, is, again, in the hands of the city itself.

Though the city must make the critical decisions, professionals or others with expert knowledge should not abandon their responsibility by withholding their opinions, nor should the state and federal governments fail to provide incentives for the development of local capability. It is recommended here that something resembling the kinds of agencies named above be established in every city that finds itself faced with problems of development and redevelopment. Furthermore, it is recommended that the capabilities and responsibilities of local social service systems be drastically upgraded. Experience in relocation has shown that these agencies are often narrowly focused, inclined toward the *status quo,* biased against those sections of the population that are difficult to identify with or serve, and suspicious of relocation agencies and other agents of societal change. Moreover, they are quite often understaffed and disorganized in their efforts. These deficiencies must be recognized by local government and the necessary corrective measures must be encouraged if the relocation agency is to get the service assistance required to mount a positive program or if the needs for service generally are to be met. In the process of strengthening the service network, a guiding objective should be to establish contact before relocation occurs and before personal crises develop. A greater decentralization of the delivery system, as in the form of neighborhood services centers, would be in line with achieving such contact.

The People's Choice

Whether there is a recognition of needs and whether there is an adequate response to them ultimately rests with the people and the institutions that represent them. Events current at the time of this writing would lead one to believe that the people are at one and the same time not anxious to act on the promises set forth in the legislation of the 1930's and 1940's and irritated with the effects of their own failure to act. In the absence of substantial enthusiasm, two possibilities exist: one is that our problems will not be solved; the other, that their solution will come accidentally and incrementally. Again, relocation is symbolic of where we stand in our commitment to the improvement of our environment and to the rectification of past injustice and present inequity in our society. Action is called for, and relocation has a positive role to play in the action.

POSITIVE RELOCATION

Throughout the preceding pages, the discussion has revolved around the recommendation that relocation become a positive component of the redevelopment process. By "positive" is meant that the status of relocation be elevated within development planning so that the housing and locational needs of the population be considered on an equal, rather than ancillary, plane with the use to which land is put; that housing and environmental needs of specific residents be given special consideration before the decision is made to displace them; that some renewal projects be initiated primarily to benefit the residents of an area; that rehousing services be available to any disadvantaged household seeking to move; and that the relocation service program be broadened and expanded so as to include extensive social services along with comprehensive housing services. The demonstration projects that were a part of the study have given us particular insights into the conduct of a service program, and it is in this area that we have been most specific in outlining what we mean by positive relocation.

As currently stated in the Urban Renewal Manual, the two objectives of relocation are:

> (1) Families and individuals displaced by a Title I project shall have the full opportunity of occupying housing that is decent,

safe and sanitary, that is within their financial means, and that is in reasonably convenient locations.

(2) Displacement shall be carried out with a minimum of hardship to site occupants.

While one could hardly argue with these goals, the tone of positive relocation that has been advocated here is missing. There is no implication in the two statements that relocation can be an important tool in improving the life situation of large numbers of people. A third objective may at least partially overcome this deficiency:

Relocation shall be carried out as a positive program designed to improve the housing and social conditions of needy households that are compelled to move by public action.

While this kind objective hardly goes far enough, it is offered here as a first step, and as a vehicle by which the resolution of the problems faced by the older residents of urban centers and others in similar circumstances can be made one of the primary goals of the whole redevelopment effort.

6

INCOMPLETE UNDERSTANDINGS

A case has been made throughout this summary report for capitalizing on the experience that has been gained and redirecting the redevelopment program toward the very obvious needs of the poor sectors of the urban population, of which those of the elderly are illustrative. A major aspect of this change in direction would be the conversion of the relocation program, narrowly conceived, into a rehousing program, broadly conceived.

Implicit in this case is the assumption that we have enough knowledge to proceed, in either incremental or dramatic ways, with justified confidence. While it would be held here that, by and large, this assumption is correct, there are still a number of areas where our knowledge is quite inadequate. The purpose of this chapter is to identify what appear to be the more important of these areas.

RESEARCH IN RELOCATION

There is some debate among authorities about what can be accomplished during the rather short relocation period. Experience with the elderly population in older urban areas, which in significant ways is representative of the total population in such areas, would suggest that relocation can usually neither harm nor help in substantial, long-range ways because of the overriding importance of more dominant factors. In some cases, however, the involuntary move can be a devastating thing in itself, and it is to these cases that further research in relocation should be addressed.

The Effects of Moving

The so-called trauma of relocation, which is connected with the difficulties that many elderly persons seem to experience, deserves considerably closer examination than it has thus far received. It was pointed out in Chapters 2 and 3 that a sudden, undesired move can be a destructive psychological blow to an older person. Much of this has to do with the fact that most older persons assume that their moving days are over. To them, their environment and present life style are often equated with life itself.[1]

The research that is proposed would further illuminate the nature of this shock and offer means of preventing its worst effects.[2] The investigation might take the form of an extended period of observation of a cross-section of an entire relocation population going through a normal relocation experience. Such things as patterns of living, relationships with other people and institutions, attitudes, adaptiveness and self-reliance would be examined over the course of the relocation process. The objectives of such a study would be to understand the relation of the nature and circumstances of relocation to its psychological ill effects, and to hypothesize what could be done to alleviate it or compensate for it.

The impression one gets from viewing the elderly in isolation is that they are probably more vulnerable to the negative or destructive aspects of moving than are their younger counterparts. Yet it is not likely that the psychologically unsettling aspects of relocation are restricted solely to the older sector of the population. While a large minority of older persons suffer a great deal in ways for which they cannot be compensated, perhaps an even larger number benefit in substantial ways from residential movement. New opportunities are presented; latent strengths are recognized; life takes on new dimensions. By the same token, many younger persons, who are assumed to be better equipped to handle and benefit from a move, probably feel the impact and disruption at least as keenly as some of their older neighbors.

What is needed is greater knowledge of what kinds of mobility are good and what kinds are bad, for what kinds of people, irrespective of age, and under what circumstances. There may be

1. See, for example, Marc Fried, "Grieving for a Lost Home," in *The Urban Condition: People and Policy in the Metropolis,* L. J. Duhl, Ed. (New York: Basic Books, 1963).

2. Some work in this direction has already begun. One excellent study on the effects of moving is that by William H. Key, *When People are Forced to Move* (The Menninger Foundation, Topeka, Kansas, 1967).

implications for redevelopment, rehousing, locational, and other choices that planners are called upon to propose that are currently overlooked altogether because of ignorance. A first step here would be to assemble the information about the nature and circumstances of residential moving that has been accumulated in social science research to date.

Two related, although somewhat subordinate, matters are the extent to which relocatees are highly mobile anyway, and the degree to which "community" has meaning for them. In many cases the younger relocatee is a recent in-migrant or has become accustomed to intracity movement. To the extent that this is true, the popular notions about the importance of "community" are not applicable, and the current resistances to renewal on the grounds of preservation of "neighborhood cohesion" cannot be accepted without further inquiry. Whatever one's expectations regarding these matters, the findings in this volume about the comparative stability of the elderly, their dependence on the familiar, and their loyalty to place should not be imputed indiscriminately to the entire populations of these areas.

The Question of Self-Relocation

It has been asserted elsewhere that a rather large proportion of the relocation population is "lost" to governmental agencies, either because households leave the site before the relocation program begins, or because they move without notice to unannounced locations. This has not been characteristic of the elderly, so it was not emphasized in this study, but it does appear to be common among younger households. The public effort to assist relocatees has been roundly criticized for not serving these lost households. It is held that, either by beginning the relocation program earlier or by searching harder, these families and individuals could be reached and assisted. It is also presumed by some that these persons are likely to be among those who are most in need of help.

These arguments are not altogether convincing. During the period between announcement and the point at which relocation services are instituted, it would be quite natural for many households simply to consummate their already made plans to move, and they would have no particularly strong reasons for staying. Furthermore, it might be quite natural for the strongest families to be among the first to leave as the area became less desirable. For others, who may simply be footloose or desirous of anonymity, an early move may also be natural and may not necessarily imply weakness or social pathology. In order to establish the relative size of these groups, a closer examination of the households that are lost to the relocation agency is in order. It is quite obvious that if the matter of lost cases is accepted as worthy of serious investigation, it will be necessary to survey a renewal area in advance of announcement.

The Loss of Business or Employment

Among those on whom relocation can have disastrous effects are the elderly owners of small marginal business establishments. In many cases, no attempt is made to reestablish these businesses elsewhere, and in an unknown number of additional cases reestablishment is attempted but results in failure.

Much of the concern about relocation, as reflected in the legislative changes since 1949, has centered on the plight of these and other businessmen. Efforts have thus been made to assist such businesses to renew operations after relocation, but the high incidence of mortality continues. Research should single out these business deaths and analyze the reasons for them, the effects on their owners, and what might possibly be done to compensate for the negative effects.[3]

A similar investigation should be made of workers who lose their jobs because of relocation and are unable to replace them, or whose income is drastically reduced in other ways attributable to relocation. In the case of the elderly businessman or employee whose livelihood and life style are seriously threatened by relocation, additional assistance and compensation seems desirable. In some cases this might take the form of substantial severance pay over an extended period of time. Many of these enterprises and jobs are the result of long years of struggle in finding a satisfactory and secure place in the urban economy, and a new and rapid adaptation at an advanced age is entirely too much for society to expect.

3. Again, the literature is deficient but not wholly absent. See the work of W. N. Kinnard and Z. S. Malinowski, *The Impact of Dislocation from Urban Renewal Areas on Small Business* (Storrs: University of Connecticut, 1960).

Financial and Social Dependency

Discussions of the position of the elderly in our society inevitably lead to questions of "useful role" and "dependency." These are questions on which research has just recently begun to focus, although the terms themselves have been in our vocabulary for some time. The problem of the proper role of the older person in our society is a real one, but a long-range one. For the elderly who presently reside in older urban areas, the more pressing need is not for ways of being creatively involved, but simply for means of subsisting and meeting basic personal needs and desires. The stigma of poverty and the subordinate position of the elderly combine to deprive many of our urban elderly of all but a mean existence. As was said earlier, the degree to which members of this population—and many of its younger counterparts, especially if they are members of minority groups—can lead satisfying lives is largely a function of the amount of help society is willing to give and the manner in which the help is dispensed. The important immediate question is thus how to provide them with sustenance without threatening their last traces of dignity and self-esteem.

The most relevant research need in this context is to discover the degree to which relocation can serve as a means of producing instant and dramatic evidence that the older person is considered to have worth and is deserving of a certain amount of opportunity in establishing a satisfactory life for himself. If relocation benefits were substantial, and rehousing choices adequate, a great deal might be accomplished in this direction. Furthermore, the offer of aid at the time of relocation might be interpreted by both the individual and society as a whole as a right rather than a patronizing handout. Two issues worthy of investigation, then, are the amount of financial and other assistance necessary to give an elderly household a minimum of independence and security, and the extent to which a technique such as relocation is qualitively superior to some other vehicle and more acceptable both for the individual and to the general society for accomplishing that end. Furthermore, while they are raised with specific reference to the elderly, the same issues have relevance for other deprived households as well.

THE HOUSING MARKET

It has been observed here and in other works on redevelopment policy that the greatest impediment to successful physical relocation is the insufficient supply of good housing. While there is no longer a serious housing shortage for most groups in the population, lower-income families still find it very much with them. The welfare of particular groups could be substantially raised simply by increasing the overall pace of net additions to the housing supply. While this is a general and long-range issue, it is raised here as a basis for research because of its obvious bearing on the relocation problem.

The Adequacy of Existing Vacancies

In dealing with this issue, one quite definite need is for an exploration into the degree to which existing vacancies in the relevant rent and price classes are sufficient to absorb the relocation demand. Questions that arise here have to do with the quality and location of the vacant stock compared with that of the occupied stock within the same class, the extent to which a reasonable degree of choice is afforded the relocation population by one vacancy rate as opposed to another, and the overall adequacy of the vacancy rate for gauging the effects that additional demand will have on housing prices and rents. In the early 1950's, when redevelopment programs involving relocation first assumed large proportions, the market was somewhat tighter at the lower end than it is today. It might therefore appear that the meaning that can be drawn from the vacancy rate is less significant than it was at that time, but this is at least partially offset by the fact that the quantity of annual relocation is substantially greater now than it was a decade ago.

Relocation: Criteria for Success

If a novice observer were to read the goals of the Housing Act of 1949, he would probably surmise that the site resident was intended to be a major beneficiary of redevelopment, rather than a relocatee. Subsequent experience with both the urban renewal and highway programs has made it obvious that those dislodged are not a primary beneficiary, but that they should be, and that they will have to be if redevelopment programs are to be fully effective and allowed to move forward at a rapid pace. One way of attempting to measure the success of relocation as a rehousing program would be to allow an independent investigator to establish how a given relocation population "ought" to be housed before relocation actually takes place, and then to compare what in fact happens with the preestablished "ought." At present, no such standards are established, beyond the insistence on specific physical conditions and generalities about location and environment. As a result, it has been difficult to assess the degree to which the goal of "a decent home in a suitable living environment" has been achieved by relocation. As was said in Chapter 5, some administrators have tended to define success as what actually happened, and on the other hand, some "objective" observers have tended toward excessive criticism and even cynicism instead of offering better ways of evaluating success.

Such questions as these, of course, leave one with the notion that perhaps the "ought" is not clearly enough established in the literature on housing for it to be offered as a standard. This is probably less true than it would appear. The necessity is not so much to develop greater knowledge of housing needs, but rather to apply what knowledge we do have to the relevant population groups. In the case of the elderly, for example, such notions as "modified independence," "residential concentrations," "hominess," and "proximity to facilities," have been expressed in previous pages of this report. There is no reason why such criteria as these cannot be made operational in specific cases, thus allowing for eventual measures of success in achieving satisfactory relocation housing. Similar notions have been posited for the single male population and for other special groups, and are probably not any more difficult to apply than those established for the elderly.

One valid criterion for success might be that the disadvantaged sector of the relocation population was relocated into housing like that in which the households in the next highest income brackets now find themselves. In this way, it would be possible to determine whether any real change in the distribution of wealth or income had taken place, which in the last analysis is what most social programs are ostensibly designed to promote. If the results showed, for example, that the relocation housing resembled what had been occupied *before* relocation, it would be quite obvious that no absolute improvement had been made, and that the relocatees had probably suffered a relative slippage in well-being compared with the new occupants of the redevelopment site.

Comparative Housing Needs

In the long run, even such studies as the ones just suggested will be inadequate to the task. What we really need to know is considerably more complex than the mere recitation of the housing needs of particular groups. Such questions as the following need to be answered, at least in a tentative manner: To what kinds of people is proximity to other kinds an important consideration? For what kinds of people are given areas particularly well suited? What things are valued more highly by one group than another? How should groups be classified for the study of housing demand and need?

The fields of land economics, urban sociology, civic design, and other relevant disciplines have not yet provided answers sufficient to derive rational population distribution patterns for urban areas. As was just observed, some work has been done on the preferences or needs of particular groups, but no comparative analysis has been undertaken that would begin to show how important it is to one set of individuals as opposed to another to achieve a given amount of space or to be located in specific proximity to another group or to a certain facility.

The point is that, without more refined knowledge of needs, preferences, and the suitability of alternative housing packages for the various demographic sectors, we cannot be sure if our present course is the right one. Only after these are approximated can adequate answers be given to the question, "Who can benefit most from living where?" An attempt to deal in greater depth with housing and locational requirements would thus be in order. Then the term "maximization of satisfaction" will have some meaning as a social policy, and it will be possible to establish the amount of subsidy that such a goal will require in any choice situation.

Closely associated with the need to explore underlying needs and preferences is the problem of the variation in the amount and proportion of income spent for housing. There is such a wide variation, even among households in the same income groups, that one is led to question whether there is something wrong with the classification scheme itself. In some cases, the variation may be due to transitory matters or simply to deficiencies in the data, but in others it may be a matter of real differences in attitudes and needs, or of fundamental malfunctioning in the way housing is distributed. In any case, a major effort ought to be undertaken to explicate the term "housing preference" and to relate it to ways in which it is expressed or thwarted.

Still another relationship, that between housing quality and housing cost, would seem to need a greater degree of attention than has thus far been given it. It is common knowledge that postrelocation housing quality, at least in a limited physical sense, has been generally superior to prerelocation quality. It is also true that housing costs are generally higher after relocation, so a relationship between the two is implied. It is not known, however, whether relocatees are getting their "money's worth" or indeed what that term really means except in a limited market sense. That a poor family has to pay, say, $70 per month or 30 percent of its income to have any house at all is not adequate to define what that house is worth to them, given their other desires and the demands put upon them by other necessities. The institutional conditions that prevent the price of the house from falling below $70 would satisfy neither the welfare economist nor the individual himself. Nor will it be practically possible to operate a broad-scale program of housing subsidies until we have a better means of determining the "worth" of a given type of unit to a given type of household, or the worth to society of having its population more satisfactorily housed. Again, these problems are hardly new, but they do take on additional meaning when viewed from the standpoint of relocation policy.

RENEWAL POLICY

The most challenging—and elusive—demand for city planning research emerges from the clash of housing and nonhousing goals in redevelopment. It behooves the student of urban systems to develop, first, a means of determining the best use to which different parcels of land should be put, and second, a means of determining what distribution of the population will insure maximum satisfaction. As things now stand, redevelopment is focused on nonhousing goals (even when new housing is a part of the renewal plan) and there is no parallel public effort of an equivalent magnitude to achieve a proper spatial distribution of people or an improvement in their level of housing well being. Goals concerning efficiency, the tax base, beauty and civic pride, and service to influential groups are common, and even these are not always based on the best theoretical or empirical evidence. But the comparative needs of different people for accessibility, convenience, amenity, and security have hardly, if at all, been brought to bear on major redevelopment decisions.

Substantial support should thus be given to research that would attempt to identify the locational and other needs of the various sectors of the population and to reconcile conflicting needs in an equitable manner. Once begun, such results as there are will then begin to influence the manner in which the population is in fact housed, and conflicts between residential and other goals can be identified and resolved in advance of their actual occurrence.

Model Cities

Whether rational population planning is a real possibility or not, it is quite clear that greater weight must be given to the housing aspects of the renewal program. One means by which a two-pronged approach to redevelopment, such as the one suggested here, could be at least partially tested is through the Model Cities mechanism. In at least one model city, it might be feasible to establish a program whereby a complete integration of the rehousing aspects of renewal with its land use objectives is attempted. Returning to the principle of equivalent replacement, a program for the enlargement of the housing supply would accompany every redevelopment program involving displacement. Whether the replacement units were built on-site or off, their character and cost would have to be consistent with the needs and financial capacity of the site occupants. Needless to say, only a portion (probably a substantial portion) of the site occupants would themselves move directly into the newly available stock, but presumably their counterparts in other areas would avail themselves of the new opportunities to an extent that would result in sufficient alternatives for the balance of site occupants.

A program such as this would be proper as a demonstration on many grounds, but perhaps the most important is that it would allow for a degree of flexibility in the development of programs and a degree of costly coordination, work programming, and scheduling beyond that which has customarily been characteristic of redevelopment and housing programs or indeed possible under these programs. As a demonstration, and thereby as something of a research endeavor, a great deal could be learned about the administrative feasibility of such an obviously desirable approach, and peripheral information on the relative value of specific housing programs in serving the poverty groups could be gained as well.

Social Integration of the Population

The effects of relocation on the receiving neighborhood are sometimes held to be important, but often overlooked, aspects of relocation. The elderly person who cannot maintain his home in a condition compatible with the residences around it and the younger family with boisterous children are both felt to be deleterious influences on otherwise good areas. Blame for "the spread of slums" is at least partially laid at the feet of relocation.

If all of the poor areas were cleared at once, a certain amount of harm would surely be done to the receiving neighborhoods, because of overcrowding, if for no other reason. Redevelopment, however, has proceeded at such a slow pace that it is difficult to conceive that great harm has been done. Moreover, insofar as relocatees are actually quite similar to the occupants of the receiving neighborhoods, the "spread of slums" argument loses even more of its emotional force. What is perhaps needed is an investigation into the characteristics of typical areas of reception, and a comparison of the numbers and types of relocatees with the numbers and types among the stable population. Only then can we begin to judge whether the supposed effects are substantial—or, indeed, whether relocatees with socially undesirable qualities do in fact usually move to better areas.

It is held by an increasing number of liberals that the dispersal of minority and otherwise socially handicapped families is inherently not a bad but a good thing, for both the mover and the receiving neighborhood. If this is true, the limited amount of change necessitated by relocation might on balance be something not to be discouraged, but to be encouraged. The positive and negative aspects have yet to be fully explored, but it would be useful to survey a region with an eye to the identification of areas that are amenable to gradual racial and social change, and to offer programs that would effect such change.

Whether renewal perpetuates, accentuates, or reduces segregation, especially through the results of its relocation policies, is an issue of considerable importance. It would also be appropriate for a team of demographers, economists, and sociologists to undertake a project which would specify what immediate and full integration would really mean, spatially and socially, what programs would be necessary to bring it about, whether the black community feels it can in fact benefit from integration on a large scale, or whether it will be necessary for the black community to establish itself largely as a separate community before integration becomes possible. Such research could provide the various concerned parties with the facts regarding the limitations on the achievement of their goals.

As long as most of the desirable neighborhoods are effectively closed to nonwhites, no effort to achieve an equitable distribution of the housing supply will be completely successful. Furthermore, as long as relocation loads continue to be dominated by non-whites, the clash of irresistible force and immovable object will be intensified. Majority groups will reluctantly admit some minorities, but will continue to resist or flee. It may well be that ways will have to be found to create a substantially separate inventory of new housing for nonwhites if decent accommodations for them are to become a reality. In many cities, by the 1980's, more than half of the population will be nonwhite, and a few entire cities may have become "Negro ghettos." If we are to achieve a substantial degree of equity by that time, research and action might have to be directed toward the reconstruction of entire areas for the present residents of the city, or the massive decanting of these residents to entirely new towns. Research into these questions would, as a matter of course, have to deal with relocation as it contributes to the extension or disintegration of the racial ghetto.

The Uses of Relocation Data

The use of data in the course of this study suggests that available material has not yet been fully exploited in determining local and national housing needs and in establishing programs qualitatively and quantitatively adequate to meet these needs. It is probably true that the bulk of the urban poverty population presently resides within potential renewal areas or other similar areas, and that their characteristics and problems of adaptation are similar to those of persons who have already been relocated. Hence, it would make good sense to use the descriptions of local relocation workloads as one basis for determining the nature and size of the programs necessary for solving the urban housing problem. While rough estimates have been made many times, even the various community renewal programs have failed to describe the needy population and the size of the task in realistic detail, and at the federal level there has been little serious use of relocation data for these purposes.

An intimate knowledge of the relocation population in a given city can also be helpful in determining the extent to which the social service network is adequately doing its job. Individual cases of relocation often uncover families who are eligible for or in need of aid of one kind or another but who are not receiving it. Compilations or summaries of many such situations can provide the basis for estimating city-wide needs and can thus lend support to appeals for more public money and the training of professional personnel.

Related to the kind of work outlined in the preceding paragraphs would be greater attention to the projection of urban social needs and the development of more refined techniques for their measurement and projection. Knowing, for example, the current number of elderly urban households suffering under one form of deprivation or another is hardly the same thing as estimating the extent of the same condition for a future year. Such projections would be comparable with, although more complex than, the construction of life expectancy tables based on cohort experience rather than on the experience of a population at one moment in time. The use of cohort techniques in projecting the extent and nature of social problems and so-called social pathology would seem to hold great promise on a number of counts. Besides giving a more realistic prognosis of the particular social ill, cohort methods would almost automatically allow for greater insight into the societal causes of those ills, which ones are inevitable, whether some are reversible, which ones are chronic and progressive, which ones are acute and temporary, and particularly which ones are contagious.

The importance of the cohort approach to the projection of social problems is quite clear from this study of the urban elderly population, but it would hardly be honest to claim that the idea is new. It remains, however, for a major attempt to be made that will assemble data for large numbers of cohorts, and this step may be the crucial one for policy purposes. By viewing the experience of one cohort relative to its starting point, and applying that pattern of change to the younger cohort, we can begin to make more accurate statements about future conditions, the size and nature of necessary programs, and the most critical points of susceptibility to permanently corrective action. The main point is that cross-sectional studies may lead to cause-effect statements for a given cohort, but comparative studies of several cohorts is necessary before such statements can be tested and generalized, before the relationships can be measured, or before reasonable projections can be set down.

What Skills Are Needed?

With great frequency it is heard that successful relocation requires maximum coordination among the relevant social agencies. This particular study has hardly refuted the general imperative; in fact, it has carried the imperative to a second level. What we need to know now, and what we recognize as a necessity because of the problems associated with relocation, is the nature of the academic skills and professional disciplines that should be represented on the "team" that does the redevelopment planning. A decade and a half of urban renewal have demonstrated that land use planners alone are not equipped to do the job. A research endeavor worthy of support, then, would be one which would deal with the question of the degree to which physical planning as it has been known is still relevant, and the extent to which some form of broader planning should supplant it. The Model Cities program will surely shed some light here but an intellectual endeavor is also required, to work in parallel and push ahead of the incremental knowledge that comes with administrative experience.

Political Power

There is a definite need to undertake a study in depth of the political power of the elderly population as a whole and of the urban poor in particular. The present study attempted to make a beginning in this direction, but any conclusive study would have to focus on the poverty population generally. The antipoverty war may have opened the door to such an effort. Until the results are in, it remains a moot question whether and by whom the interests of the poor—particularly the elderly poor, who are among those who are farthest from the mainstream—will or should be represented.

If the middle-aged and elderly urban residents do not receive a substantial amount of assistance during the ensuing decade or two, by the 1980's a substantial proportion of all households in our older central cities may be headed by impoverished elderly Negroes. The generations that become old in the 1990's or later will probably be considerably stronger and more financially able, but such will not be the case for the millions that reach old age before them. In the face of this bleak prospect, political power may be decisive.

IN CONCLUSION

The research and innovative field work that were undertaken in the course of this study proved to be useful in identifying a number of changes in the relocation process that would be beneficial to the elderly households and businesses that are affected. Also identified, however, were necessary changes of a much broader scope and of a much greater moment, changes that need no research to identify them. Thus it remains the principal "finding" of this effort and others like it that rather massive changes are necessary in the allocation and distribution of the nation's resources before any of the more subtle needs have any chance of being fully satisfied. The situation that is sought is one in which investigations into relocation will be hardly more than of historic interest because the social welfare system will have long since assured each person an adequate share in the nation's wealth and a claim to the opportunities and supports he might need to sustain himself through periods of shock or adversity.